IN TIME OF WAR

IN TIME OF WAR

IN TIME OF WAR

War Poetry selected by ANNE HARVEY

Blackie

British Library Cataloguing in Publication Data

In time of war.
 1. Children's poetry, English
 I. Harvey, Anne
 821′.912′0809282   PR1195.C47

 ISBN 0-216-92103-1
 ISBN 0-216-92102-3 Pbk

 Educational Edition ISBN 0-216-92324-7

Blackie and Son Ltd
7 Leicester Place
London WC2H 7BP
and
Bishopbriggs
Glasgow G64 2NZ

Printed in Great Britain by Thomson Litho

CONTENTS

For my mother
Rose Lewis
and in memory of my father
Charles Lewis
They lived through both World Wars

INTRODUCTION

When I was asked to edit a collection of war poetry for young people I had mixed feelings. At first the challenge excited me, then I suffered doubts about the wisdom of offering young readers poetry on such a bleak subject. Why not put past wars behind us and concentrate on making the world a peaceful place?

Tentatively, I broached the idea to some teacher friends, a librarian, some children: the response was encouraging. Both world wars were taught in Junior and Middle Schools, with class projects mounted on warfare and the Home Front. But war poetry itself wasn't actually introduced until pupils were older, in the senior school, and working for public examinations.

In 1986 the Imperial War Museum's Education Department invited me to present some Second World War programmes to visiting schools. I took along a group of actors and we offered a collage of songs, poems, documentary material and scenes from books. The school audiences showed an intelligent response: there was lively discussion afterwards and questions. I decided then and there I would go ahead with the anthology.

Once the War Poets meant for me just Rupert Brooke, Wilfred Owen, and Siegfried Sassoon. They symbolized the 1914–18 War and we 'did' them in English Literature at school. I, along with twenty-five or so other girls in gym tunics, was carried away by Brooke's shining patriotism, Owen's scenes of trench horror, Sassoon's bitter edged sarcasm. They appear in this anthology along with others I came to know later—Edward Thomas, Ivor Gurney, Charles Sorley, Isaac Rosenberg, Robert Graves and more.

7

I haven't set out to provide an academic or critical selection of what I, personally, consider the finest writing. Amongst the poems are anonymous verses and songs. It seemed to me that choice should echo the moods of war: patriotism and pacifism, enthusiasm and disillusionment. Patriotic feeling was high in August 1914. Men were urged to join up. 'YOUR COUNTRY NEEDS YOU!' 'WOMEN OF BRITAIN SAY GO' cried the posters. White feathers were handed to men not in uniform, often quite unfairly, by jingoistic women, and young girls were envious of brothers who could enlist and had 'all the luck!'. This fervour was quickly dampened. On the first day of the Somme Battle alone there were 60,000 casualties, and the final total of dead and wounded during the Great War numbered millions. Fathers of families, boys scarcely out of school, brothers, sons, husbands, lovers. They were to be known as the Lost Generation.

In 1981 a collection of women's war poetry and verse was published. This was a revelation. Yes, a few poems by women were certainly known, but women war poets in quantity were unheard of. They were brought to light by the books' editor, Catherine Reilly, who, while researching for a bibliography of First World War Poets, discovered that of the 2,225 poets writing, 532—one quarter—were women.

There is no doubt that war prompts people to write, to record their experiences; servicemen and women as well as civilians, professional writers and amateurs. The very threat of conflict, separation, hardship and death heightens the emotions.

The first part of *In Time of War* closes in 1919 with Sassoon—one of the few poets who survived the war—remembering: 'the rats and the stench of corpses rotting in front of the front-line trench', and questioning: 'Do you ever stop and ask "Is it all going to happen again"?'

Twenty years later, in 1939, thirteen year old Elizabeth Jennings heard the announcement 'This country is at war with Germany' on the wireless and later recalled in a poem:

> I was afraid for I did not know what this meant . . . War
> On that September Sunday made us feel frightened
>   Of what our world waited for.

And it began all over again. A longer war this time and spread over many countries—Europe, North Africa, and the Far East, with fighting on a far greater scale by land, sea and air. Women were more actively involved and so were civilians.

There was widespread devastation to towns and cities, and air-raids accounted for major loss of life. I was six when war broke out and many memories are clear: having to be quiet when news was broadcast; my parents' constant reminder of 'Ssh! Mr Churchill's speaking'; ration books for food and clothes; and never enough sweets. We queued for everything—once almost a whole day for sandals at Lilley and Skinner in Oxford Street. I remember a disgusting dried egg and damp cabbage meal at the British Restaurant where my mother did her war work for the Womens' Voluntary Service. When my father joined the British Army Intelligence Corps and went to France and Germany, it was our first family parting. We were evacuated for a while to Cornwall, but came home again to barrage-balloons in the sky, black-out at the windows, the constant sirens and the night time excitement of the air raid shelter. There were rhymes and cartoons about Hitler, and at the end the last All Clear and dancing round the Victory bonfire waving a Union Jack.

The three foremost poets of the war, Alun Lewis, Keith Douglas, and Sidney Keyes, all died on active service. One poem, John Pudney's 'For Johnny', reached the hearts of millions of film-goers when it was featured in *The Way to the Stars*. Yet, somehow, the fine mainstream of World War Two poetry has remained in the shadows. 'Who are the Second World War Poets?' is a frequent question. I've tried to answer it in part here, again helped by Catherine Reilly's further research into women's poetry, and again using songs, slogans and popular verse as part of the picture. The Imperial War Museum is a mine of information on art and literature as well as being a very good place for discovering more about all aspects of both World Wars. I would like to thank Dr Christopher Dowling for his support over this book, Anita Ballin and Robert Jackson in the Education Department and Jenny Wood and Robin Hamilton for their help with illustrative material.

I can't emphasize enough how Catherine Reilly's research has added interest not just to this book, but to my radio and theatre programmes on war literature. Her friendship and advice have been invaluable, and I thank her warmly.

Anne Harvey
London 1987

THE
FIRST WORLD WAR

THE GREAT WAR

Whenever war is spoken of
I find
The war that was called Great invades the mind:
The grey militia marches over land
A darker mood of grey
Where fractured tree-trunks stand
And shells, exploding, open sudden fans
Of smoke and earth.
Blind murders scythe
The deathscape where the iron brambles writhe;
The sky at night
Is honoured with rosettes of fire,
Flares that define the corpses on the wire
As terror ticks on wrists at zero hour.
These things I see,
But they are only part
Of what it is that slyly probes the heart:
Less vivid images and words excite
The sensuous memory
And, even as I write,
Fear and a kind of love collaborate
To call each simple conscript up
For quick inspection:
Trenches' parapets
Paunchy with sandbags; bandoliers, tin-hats,
Candles in dug-outs,
Duckboards, mud and rats.
Then, like patrols, tunes creep into the mind:
A long long trail The Rose of No-Man's Land,
Home Fires and *Tipperary*;
And through the misty keening of a band
Of Scottish pipes the proper names are heard
Like fateful commentary of distant guns:
Passchendaele, Bapaume, and Loos, and Mons.
And now,
Whenever the November sky
Quivers with a bugle's hoarse, sweet cry,
The reason darkens; in its evening gleam
Crosses and flares, tormented wire, grey earth
Splattered with crimson flowers,

And I remember,
Not the war I fought in
But the one called Great
Which ended in a sepia November
Four years before my birth.

Vernon Scannell

1914

War broke: and now the Winter of the world
With perishing great darkness closes in.
The foul tornado, centred at Berlin,
Is over all the width of Europe whirled,
Rending the sails of progress. Rent or furled
Are all Art's ensigns. Verse wails. Now begin
Famines of thought and feeling. Love's wine's thin.
The grain of human Autumn rots, down-hurled.

For after Spring had bloomed in early Greece,
And Summer blazed her glory out with Rome,
An Autumn softly fell, a harvest home,
A slow grand age, and rich with all increase.
But now, for us, wild Winter, and the need
Of sowings for new Spring, and blood for seed.

Wilfred Owen

PEACE

Now, God be thanked Who has matched us with His hour,
　　And caught our youth, and wakened us from sleeping,
With hand made sure, clear eye, and sharpened power,
　　To turn, as swimmers into cleanness leaping,
Glad from a world grown old and cold and weary,
　　Leave the sick hearts that honour could not move,
And half-men, and their dirty songs and dreary,
　　And all the little emptiness of love!

Oh! we, who have known shame, we have found release there,
　　Where there's no ill, no grief, but sleep has mending,
　　　Naught broken save this body, lost but breath;
Nothing to shake the laughing heart's long peace there
　　But only agony, and that has ending;
　　　And the worst friend and enemy is but Death.

　　　Rupert Brooke

　　　Oh, we don't want to lose you
　　　But we think you ought to go,
　　　For your King and your Country
　　　Both need you so;
　　　We shall want you and miss you,
　　　But with all our might and main
　　　We shall cheer you, thank you, kiss you,
　　　When you come back again.

AUGUST 5. 1914

1 D.

BRITAIN

AT

WAR

THE SOLDIER

If I should die, think only this of me:
   That there's some corner of a foreign field
That is for ever England. There shall be
   In that rich earth a richer dust concealed;
A dust whom England bore, shaped, made aware,
   Gave, once, her flowers to love, her ways to roam
A body of England's, breathing English air,
   Washed by the rivers, blest by suns of home.

And think, this heart, all evil shed away,
   A pulse in the eternal mind, no less
     Gives somewhere back the thoughts by England given;
Her sights and sounds; dreams happy as her day;
   And laughter, learnt of friends; and gentleness,
     In hearts at peace, under an English heaven.

    Rupert Brooke

Goodbye, Dolly, I must leave you,
Though it breaks my heart to go.
Something tells me I am needed
At the front to fight the foe.
See the soldier boys are marching,
And I can no longer stay,
Hark! I hear the bugle calling
Goodbye, Dolly Gray!

NO ONE CARES LESS THAN I

'No one cares less than I,
Nobody knows but God,
Whether I am destined to lie
Under a foreign clod,'
Were the words I made to the bugle call in the morning.

But laughing, storming, scorning,
Only the bugles know
What the bugles say in the morning,
And they do not care, when they blow
The call that I heard and made words to early this morning.

Edward Thomas

AN IRISH AIRMAN FORESEES HIS DEATH

I know that I shall meet my fate
Somewhere among the clouds above;
Those that I fight I do not hate,
Those that I guard I do not love;
My country is Kiltartan Cross,
My countrymen Kiltartan's poor,
No likely end could bring them loss
Or leave them happier than before.
Nor law, nor duty bade me fight,
Nor public men, nor cheering crowds,
A lonely impulse of delight
Drove to this tumult in the clouds;
I balanced all, brought all to mind,
The years to come seemed waste of breath,
A waste of breath the years behind
In balance with this life, this death.

W. B. Yeats

MANGEL-WURZELS

Last year I was hoeing,
Hoeing mangel-wurzels,
Hoeing mangel-wurzels all day in the sun,
Hoeing for the squire
Down in Gloucestershire,
Willy-nilly till the sweaty job was done.

Now I'm in the 'wurzels,
In the mangel-wurzels,
All day in the 'wurzels 'neath the Belgian sun:
But among this little lot
It's a different job I've got—
For you don't hoe mangel-wurzels with a gun.

Wilfrid Gibson

RENDEZVOUS

I have a rendezvous with Death
At some disputed barricade,
When Spring comes back with rustling shade
And apple-blossoms fill the air—
I have a rendezvous with Death
When Spring brings back blue days and fair.

It may be he shall take my hand
And lead me into his dark land
And close my eyes and quench my breath—
It may be I shall pass him still.
I have a rendezvous with Death
On some scarred slope of battered hill,
When Spring comes round again this year
And the first meadow-flowers appear.

God knows 'twere better to be deep
Pillowed in silk and scented down,
Where love throbs out in blissful sleep,
Pulse nigh to pulse, and breath to breath,
Where hushed awakenings are dear . . .
But I've a rendezvous with Death
At midnight in some flaming town,
When Spring trips north again this year,
And I to my pledged word am true,
I shall not fail that rendezvous.

Alan Seeger

SOLDIERS

Brother,
I saw you on a muddy road
in France
pass by with your battalion,
rifle at the slope, full marching order,
arm swinging;
and I stood at ease,
folding my hands over my rifle,
with my battalion.
You passed me by, and our eyes met.
We had not seen each other since the days
we climbed the Devon hills together:
our eyes met, startled;
and, because the order was Silence,
we dared not speak.

O face of my friend,
alone distinct of all that company,
you went on, you went on,
into the darkness;
and I sit here at my table,
holding back my tears,
with my jaw set and my teeth clenched,
knowing I shall not be
even so near you as I saw you
in my dream.

F. S. Flint

NINETEEN-FIFTEEN

On a ploughland hill against the sky,
Over the barley, over the rye,
Time, which is now a black pine tree,
Holds out his arms and mocks at me—

'In the year of your Lord nineteen-fifteen
The acres are ploughed and the acres are green,
And the calves and the lambs and the foals are born,
But man the angel is all forlorn.

The cropping cattle, the swallow's wing,
The wagon team and the pasture spring,
Move in their seasons and are most wise,
But man, whose image is in the skies,

Who is master of all, whose hand achieves
The church and the barn and the homestead eaves—
How are the works of his wisdom seen
In the year of your Lord nineteen-fifteen?'

John Drinkwater

THE FALLING LEAVES

November 1915

Today, as I rode by,
I saw the brown leaves dropping from their tree
In a still afternoon,
When no wind whirled them whistling to the sky,
But thickly, silently,
They fell, like snowflakes wiping out the noon;
And wandered slowly thence
For thinking of a gallant multitude
Which now all withering lay,
Slain by no wind of age or pestilence,
But in their beauty strewed
Like snowflakes falling on the Flemish clay.

Margaret Postgate Cole

MANY SISTERS TO MANY BROTHERS

When we fought campaigns (in the long Christmas rains)
　　With soldiers spread in troops on the floor,
I shot as straight as you, my losses were as few,
　　My victories as many, or more.
And when in naval battle, amid cannon's rattle,
　　Fleet met fleet in the bath,
My cruisers were as trim, my battleships as grim,
　　My submarines cut as swift a path.
Or, when it rained too long, and the strength of the strong
　　Surged up and broke a way with blows,
I was as fit and keen, my fists hit as clean,
　　Your black eye matched my bleeding nose.
Was there a scrap or ploy in which you, the boy,
　　Could better me? You could not climb higher,
Ride straighter, run as quick (and to smoke made you sick)
. . . . But I sit here and you're under fire.

Oh, it's you that have the luck, out there in blood and muck:
　　You were born beneath a kindly star;
All we dreamt, I and you, you can really go and do,
　　And I can't, the way things are.
In a trench you are sitting, while I am knitting
　　A hopeless sock that never gets done.
Well, here's luck, my dear;—and you've got it, no fear;
　　But for me . . . a war is poor fun.

Rose Macaulay

22

THE LEVELLER

Near Martinpuich that night of Hell
Two men were struck by the same shell,
Together tumbling in one heap
Senseless and limp like slaughtered sheep.

One was a pale eighteen-year-old,
Blue-eyed and thin and not too bold,
Pressed for the war not ten years too soon,
The shame and pity of his platoon.

The other came from far-off lands
With bristling chin and whiskered hands,
He had known death and hell before
In Mexico and Ecuador.

Yet in his death this cut-throat wild
Groaned 'Mother! Mother!' like a child,
While that poor innocent in man's clothes
Died cursing God with brutal oaths.

Old Sergeant Smith, kindest of men,
Wrote out two copies, there and then
Of his accustomed funeral speech
To cheer the womenfolk of each:—

'He died a hero's death: and we
His Comrades of 'A' Company
Deeply regret his death: we shall
All deeply miss so dear a pal.'

Robert Graves

WINTER WARFARE

Colonel Cold strode up the Line
   (tabs of rime and spurs of ice);
stiffened all that met his glare:
   horses, men, and lice.

Visited a forward post,
   left them burning, ear to foot;
fingers stuck to biting steel,
   toes to frozen boot.

Stalked on into No Man's Land,
   turned the wire to fleecy wool,
iron stakes to sugar sticks
   snapping at a pull.

Those who watched with hoary eyes
   saw two figures gleaming there;
Hauptmann Kälte, Colonel Cold,
   gaunt in the grey air.

Stiffly, tinkling spurs they moved,
   glassy-eyed, with glinting heel
stabbing those who lingered there
   torn by screaming steel.

Edgell Rickword

THE DUG-OUT

Why do you lie with your legs ungainly huddled,
And one arm bent across your sullen, cold,
Exhausted face? It hurts my heart to watch you,
Deep-shadow'd from the candle's guttering gold;
And you wonder why I shake you by the shoulder;
Drowsy, you mumble and sigh and turn your head . . .
You are too young to fall asleep for ever;
And when you sleep you remind me of the dead.

Siegfried Sassoon

ASSAULT

Gas!
faces turned,
eyes scanned the sky,
hands feverishly ripped open canisters,
and masks were soon covering faces.
A man choked
as the white cloud,
swirling round him like fog, caught him
unawares.
Then his body flopped over.
Shells floated across
as if suspended by hidden strings,
and then, tired,
they sank earthwards.

A command!
I fixed my bayonet,
scrambled over the open trench
and struggled through
the thick pasty mud.

It was quiet
as we walked
except for the sucking,
groaning, squelching sound
which came from the wet earth
as it tried
to creep into our stockings.
The wind cut me.

Over the wall!
Then a whistle.
'Good luck, mates.'
Mind that hole. Through the wire.
Over the top.
And kill.
'God. This is fun!'

Erno Muller

AFTER THE SALVO

Up and down, up and down,
They go, the gray rat, and the brown.
The telegraph lines are tangled hair,
Motionless on the sullen air;
An engine has fallen on its back,
With crazy wheels, on a twisted track;
All ground to dust is the little town;
Up and down, up and down
They go, the gray rat, and the brown.
A skull, torn out of the graves nearby,
Gapes in the grass. A butterfly,
In azure iridescence new,
Floats into the world, across the dew;
Between the flow'rs. Have we lost our way,
Or are we toys of a god at play,
Who do these things on a young Spring day?

Where the salvo fell, on a splintered ledge
Of ruin, at the crater's edge,
A poppy lives: and young, and fair,
The dewdrops hang on the spider's stair,
With every rainbow still unhurt
From leaflet unto leaflet girt.

Man's house is crushed; the spider's lives:
Inscrutably He takes, and gives,
Who guards not any temple here,
Save the temple of the gossamer.

Up and down, up and down
They go, the gray rat, and the brown:
A pistol cracks: they too are dead.

The nightwind rustles overhead.

Herbert Asquith

CORPORAL STARE

Back from the line one night in June,
I gave a dinner at Béthune—
Seven courses, the most gorgeous meal
Money could buy or batman steal.
Five hungry lads welcomed the fish
With shouts that nearly cracked the dish;
Asparagus came with tender tops,
Strawberries in cream, and mutton chops.
Said Jenkins, as my hand he shook,
'They'll put this in the history book.'
We bawled church anthems IN CHORO,
Of Bethlehem and Hermon show,
With drinking songs, a mighty sound
To help the good red Pommard round.
Stories and laughter interspersed,
We drowned a long la Bassée thirst—
Trenches in June makes throats damn dry—
Then through the window suddenly,
Badges, stripes and medals all complete
We saw him stagger up the street,
Just like a live man—Corporal Stare!

    Stare! Killed last month at Festubert,
Caught on patrol near the Boche wire,
Torn horribly by machine-gun fire!
He paused, saluted smartly, grinned,
Then passed away like a puff of wind,
Leaving us blank astonishment.
The song broke, up we started, leant
Out of the window—nothing there,
Not the least shadow of Corporal Stare,
Only a quiver of smoke that showed
A fag-end dropped on the silent road.

Robert Graves

THE DANCERS

All day beneath the hurtling shells,
Before my burning eyes
Hover the dainty demoiselles—
The peacock dragonflies

Unceasingly they dart and glance
Above the stagnant stream . . .
And I am fighting here in France
As in a senseless dream—

A dream of shattering black shells
That hurtle overhead,
And dainty dancing demoiselles
Above the dreamless dead.

Wilfrid Gibson

I want to go home
I want to go home
I don't want to go to the trenches no more,
Where whizz-bangs and shrapnel they whistle and roar.
Take me back over the sea
Where the Alley Man can't get at me,
Oh my!
I don't want to die.
I want to go home.

THE TARGET

I shot him, and it had to be
One of us! 'Twas him or me.
'Couldn't be helped,' and none can blame
Me, for you would do the same.

My mother, she can't sleep for fear
Of what might be a-happening here
To me. Perhaps it might be best
To die, and set her fears at rest.

For worst is worst, and worry's done.
Perhaps he was the only son . . .
Yet God keeps still, and does not say
A word of guidance any way.

Well, if they get me, first I'll find
That boy, and tell him all my mind,
And see who felt the bullet worst,
And ask his pardon, if I durst.

All's a tangle. Here's my job.
A man might rave, or shout, or sob;
And God He takes no sort of heed.
This is a bloody mess indeed.

Ivor Gurney

MY BOY JACK

'Have you news of my boy Jack?'
  Not this tide.
'When d'you think that he'll come back?'
  Not with this wind blowing, and this tide.

'Has any one else had word of him?'
  Not this tide.
For what is sunk will hardly swim,
  Not with this wind blowing, and this tide.

'Oh, dear, what comfort can I find?'
  None this tide,
  Nor any tide,
Except he did not shame his kind—
  Not even with that wind blowing, and that tide.

Then hold your head up all the more,
  This tide,
  And every tide;
Because he was the son you bore,
  And gave to that wind blowing and that tide!

  Rudyard Kipling

SING A SONG OF WAR-TIME
(To the tune of *Sing a Song of Sixpence*)

Sing a song of War-time,
Soldiers marching by,
Crowds of people standing,
Waving them 'Good-bye'.
When the crowds are over,
Home we go to tea,
Bread and margarine to eat,
War economy!

If I ask for cake, or
Jam of any sort,
Nurse says, 'What! in War-time?
Archie, cert'nly not!'
Life's not very funny
Now, for little boys,
Haven't any money,
Can't buy any toys.

Mummie does the house-work,
Can't get any maid,
Gone to make munitions,
'Cause they're better paid,
Nurse is always busy,
Never time to play,
Sewing shirts for soldiers,
Nearly ev'ry day.

Ev'ry body's doing
Something for the War,
Girls are doing things
They've never done before,
Go as 'bus conductors,
Drive a car or van,
All the world is topsy-turvy
Since the War began.

Nina Macdonald

DAPHNE'S MUFFLER

Daphne bought some knitting needles when the War began,
Saying 'I will make a muffler for a Khaki Man.'
Patriotic Daphne sets her loyal heart aglow
On the shining needles, eighty stitches in a row.

'By the Red Cross Regulations,' dauntless Daphne cried,
'Mufflers made for soldiers must be very long and wide.'
Carefully she started, needles darting to and fro,
But from one to eighty is a long, long way to go.

Up the woollen khaki line her nimble fingers flew,
Here a stitch and there a stitch would drop away from view;
Many a one deserted or was missing from the row,
Daphne's worrying fingers found they'd not so far to go.

Daphne, when discovering the thinness of her line,
Found her stitches, like her childhood's years, but counted nine
Of that khaki row with which the muffler was begun,
Casualty lists reported missing, seventy-one.

Many months have passed away since Daphne first began
That long woollen muffler for that distant Khaki Man;
But she cries: 'I'm getting on, and it is nice to know
Neither Khaki Man nor I have got so far to go.'

Anon

SPREADING MANURE

There are forty steaming heaps in the one tree field,
  Lying in four rows of ten,
They must be all spread out ere the earth will yield
  As it should (And it won't, even then).

Drive the great fork in, fling it out wide;
  Jerk it with a shoulder throw,
The stuff must lie even, two feet on each side.
  Not in patches, but level . . . so!

When the heap is thrown you must go all round
  And flatten it out with the spade,
It must lie quite close and trim till the ground
  Is like bread spread with marmalade.

The north-east wind stabs and cuts our breaths,
  The soaked clay numbs our feet,
We are palsied like people gripped by death
  In the beating of the frozen sleet.

I think no soldier is so cold as we,
  Sitting in the frozen mud.
I wish I was out there, for it might be
  A shell would burst to heat my blood.

I wish I was out there, for I should creep
  In my dug-out and hide my head,
I should feel no cold when they lay me deep
  To sleep in a six-foot bed.

I wish I was out there, and off the open land:
  A deep trench I could just endure.
But things being other, I needs must stand
  Frozen, and spread wet manure.

  Rose Macaulay

34

A WAR FILM

I saw,
With a catch of the breath and the heart's uplifting,
Sorrow and pride,
 The 'week's great draw'—
The Mons Retreat;
The 'Old Contemptibles' who fought, and died,
The horror and the anguish and the glory.

As in a dream,
Still hearing machine-guns rattle and shells scream,
I came out into the street.

When the day was done,
My little son
Wondered at bath-time why I kissed him so,
Naked upon my knee.
How could he know
The sudden terror that assaulted me? . . .
The body I had borne
Nine moons beneath my heart,
A part of me . . .
If, someday,
It should be taken away
To War. Tortured. Torn.
Slain.
Rotting in No Man's Land, out in the rain—
My little son . . .
Yet all those men had mothers, every one.

How should he know
Why I kissed and kissed and kissed him, crooning his name?
He thought that I was daft.
He thought it was a game,
And laughed, and laughed.

Teresa Hooley

SEARCHLIGHT

There has been no sound of guns,
No roar of exploding bombs;
But the darkness has an edge
That grits the nerves of the sleeper.

He awakens;
Nothing disturbs the stillness,
Save perhaps the light, slow flap,
Once only, of the curtain
Dim in the darkness.

Yet there is something else
That drags him from his bed;
And he stands in the darkness
With his feet cold against the floor
And the cold air round his ankles.
He does not know why,
But he goes to the window and sees
A beam of light, miles high,
Dividing the night into two before him,
Still, stark and throbbing.

The houses and gardens beneath
Lie under the snow
Quiet and tinged with purple.

There has been no sound of guns,
No roar of exploding bombs;
Only that watchfulness hidden among the snow-covered houses,
And that great beam thrusting back into heaven
The light taken from it.

F. S. Flint

THE EXECUTION OF CORNELIUS VANE

*Le combat spirituel est aussi brutal que la
bataille d'hommes; mais la vision de la
justice est le plaisir de Dieu seul.*
                              ARTHUR RIMBAUD

Arraign'd before his worldly gods
He would have said:
'I, Cornelius Vane,
A fly in the sticky web of life,
Shot away my right index finger.
I was alone, on sentry, in the chill twilight after dawn,
And the act cost me a bloody sweat.
Otherwise the cost was trivial—they had no evidence,
And I lied to the wooden fools who tried me.
When I returned from hospital
They made me a company cook:
I peel potatoes and other men fight.'

For nearly a year Cornelius peeled potatoes
And his life was full of serenity
Then the enemy broke our line
And their hosts spread over the plains
Like unleash'd beads.
Every man was taken—
Shoemakers, storemen, grooms—
And arms were given them
That they might stem the oncoming host.

Cornelius held out his fingerless hand
And remarked that he couldn't shoot.
'But you can stab,' the sergeant said,
So he fell in with the rest, and, a little group,
They marched away towards the enemy.

After an hour they halted for a rest.
They were already in the fringe of the fight:
Desultory shells fell about them,
And past them retreating gunteams
Galloped in haste.
But they must go on.

37

Wounded stragglers came down the road,
Haggard and limping
Their arms and equipment tossed away.
Cornelius Vane saw them, and his heart was beating wildly,
For he must go on.

At the next halt
He went aside to piss,
And whilst away a black shell
Burst near him:
Hot metal shrieked past his face; .
Bricks and earth descended like hail,
And the acrid stench of explosive filled his nostrils.

Cornelius pitched his body to the ground
And crouched in trembling fear.
Another shell came singing overhead,
Nowhere near.

But Cornelius sprang to his feet, his pale face set.
He willed nothing, saw nothing, only before him
Were the free open fields:
To the fields he ran.

He was still running when he began to perceive
The tranquillity of the fields
And the battle distant.
Away in the north-east were men marching on a road;
Behind were the smoke-puffs of shrapnel,
And in the west the sun declining
In a sky of limpid gold.

When night came finally
He had reached a wood.
In the thickness of the trees
The cold wind was excluded,
And here he slept a few hours.

In the early dawn
The chill mist and heavy dew
Pierced his bones and wakened him.
There was no sound of battle to be heard.

In the open fields again
The sun shone sickly through the mist
And the dew was icy to the feet.
So Cornelius ran about in that white night,
The sun's wan glare his only guide.

Coming to a canal
He ran up and down like a dog
Deliberating where to cross.
One way he saw a bridge
Loom vaguely, but approaching
He heard voices and turned about.
He went far the other way,
But growing tired before he found a crossing,
Plunged into the icy water and swam.
The water gripped with agony;
His clothes sucked the heavy water,
And as he ran again
Water oozed and squelched from his boots,
His coat dripped and his teeth chattered.

He came to a farm.
Approaching cautiously, he found it deserted.
Within he discarded his sopping uniform, dried himself and donned
Mufti he found in a cupboard.
Dark mouldy bread and bottled cider he also found
And was refreshed.

Whilst he was eating,
Suddenly,
Machine-guns opened fire not far away,
And their harsh throbbing
Darkened his soul with fear.

The sun was more golden now,
And as he went—
Always going west—
The mist grew thin.
About noon,
As he skirted the length of a wood
The warmth had triumphed and the spring day was beautiful.
Cornelius perceived with a new joy

Pale anemones and violets of the wood,
And wished that he might ever
Exist in the perception of these woodland flowers
And the shafts of yellow light that pierced
The green dusk.

Two days later
He entered a village and was arrested.
He was hungry, and the peace of the fields
Dissipated the terror that had been the strength of his will.

He was charged with desertion
And eventually tried by court-martial.

The evidence was heavy against him,
And he was mute in his own defence.
A dumb anger and a despair
Filled his soul.

He was found guilty.
Sentence: To suffer death by being shot.

The sentence duly confirmed,
One morning at dawn they led him forth.

He saw a party of his own regiment,
With rifles, looking very sad.
The morning was bright, and as they tied
The cloth over his eyes, he said to the assembly:
'What wrong have I done that I should leave these:
The bright sun rising
And the birds that sing?'

Herbert Read

"NO PRICE CAN BE TOO HIGH WHEN HONOUR AND FREEDOM ARE AT STAKE"

The Prime Minister

SUICIDE IN THE TRENCHES

I knew a simple soldier boy
Who grinned at life in empty joy,
Slept soundly through the lonesome dark,
And whistled early with the lark.

In winter trenches, cowed and glum,
With crumps and lice and lack of rum,
He put a bullet through his brain.
No one spoke of him again.

       . . . .

You smug-faced crowds with kindling eye
Who cheer when soldier lads march by,
Sneak home and pray you'll never know
The hell where youth and laughter go.

Siegfried Sassoon

CAMOUFLAGE

They tell us tales of camouflage,
The art of hiding things;
Of painted forts and bowered guns
Invisible to wings.
   Well, it's nothing new to us,
   To us, the rank and file;
   We understand this camouflage
   —We left home with a smile.

We saw the painted battleships
And earthen-coloured trains,
And planes the hue of leaden skies
And canvas-hidden lanes.
   Well, we used the magic art
   That day of anxious fears;
   We understand this camouflage
   —We laughed away your tears.

They say that scientific men
And artists of renown
Debated long on camouflage
Before they got it down.
 Well, it came right off to us,
 We didn't have to learn;
 We understood this camouflage
 —We said we'd soon return.

We understand this camouflage,
This art of hiding things;
It's what's behind a soldier's jokes
And all the songs he sings.
 Yes, it's nothing new to us,
 To us, the rank and file;
 We understand this camouflage
 —We left home with a smile.

Anon

THE LAST LAUGH

'O Jesus Christ! I'm hit,' he said; and died.
Whether he vainly cursed, or prayed indeed,
The Bullets chirped—In vain! vain! vain!
Machine-guns chuckled,—Tut-tut! Tut-tut!
And the Big Gun guffawed.

Another sighed,—'O Mother, mother! Dad!'
Then smiled, at nothing, childlike, being dead.
 And the lofty Shrapnel-cloud
 Leisurely gestured,—Fool!
 And the falling splinters tittered.

'My Love!' one moaned. Love-languid seemed his mood,
Till, slowly lowered, his whole face kissed the mud.
 And the Bayonets' long teeth grinned;
 Rabbles of Shells hooted and groaned;
 And the Gas hissed.

Wilfred Owen

BATTLE

My body seemed to burn
Salt in the sun that drenched it through and through,
Till every particle glowed clean and new
And slowly seemed to turn
To lucent amber in a world of blue . . .

I felt a sudden wrench,
A trickle of warm blood—
And found that I was sprawling in the mud
Among the dead men in the trench.

Wilfrid Gibson

'NOTHING TO REPORT'

One minute we was laughin', me an' Ted,
The next, he lay beside me grinnin'—dead.
'There's nothin' to report,' the papers said.

May Herschel Clarke

If you want to find the old battalion,
I know where they are, I know where they are,
  I know where they are.
If you want to find the old battalion,
  I know where they are—
They're hanging on the old barbed wire.
I've seen 'em, I've seen 'em,
Hanging on the old barbed wire,
I've seen 'em, I've seen 'em,
Hanging on the old barbed wire.

HIS MATE

HI-DIDDLE-DIDDLE,
The cat and the fiddle . . .

I raised my head
and saw him seated on a heap of dead,
Yelling the nursery-tune,
Grimacing at the moon . . .

And the cow jumped over the moon.
The little dog laughed to see such sport,
And the dish ran away with the spoon.

And as he stopped to snigger,
I struggled to my knees and pulled the trigger.

Wilfrid Gibson

BREAKFAST

We ate our breakfast lying on our backs
Because the shells were screeching overhead.
I bet a rasher to a loaf of bread
That Hull United would beat Halifax
When Jimmy Stainthorpe played full-back instead
Of Billy Bradford. Ginger raised his head
And cursed, and took the bet, and dropt back dead,
We ate our breakfast lying on our backs
Because the shells were screeching overhead.

Wilfrid Gibson

BREAK OF DAY IN THE TRENCHES

The darkness crumbles away—
It is the same old druid Time as ever.
Only a live thing leaps my hand—
A queer sardonic rat—
As I pull the parapet's poppy
To stick behind my ear.
Droll rat, they would shoot you if they knew
Your cosmopolitan sympathies.
Now you have touched this English hand
You will do the same to a German—
Soon, no doubt, if it be your pleasure
To cross the sleeping green between.
It seems you inwardly grin as you pass
Strong eyes, fine limbs, haughty athletes
Less chanced than you for life,
Bonds to the whims of murder,
Sprawled in the bowels of the earth,
The torn fields of France.
What do you see in our eyes
At the shrieking iron and flame
Hurled through still heavens?
What quaver—what heart aghast?
Poppies whose roots are in man's veins
Drop, and are ever dropping;
But mine in my ear is safe,
Just a little white with the dust.

Isaac Rosenberg

TO GERMANY

You are blind like us. Your hurt no man designed,
And no man claimed the conquest of your land.
But gropers both through fields of thought confined
We stumble and we do not understand.
You only saw your future bigly planned,
And we, the tapering paths of our own mind,
And in each other's dearest ways we stand,
And hiss and hate. And the blind fight the blind.

When it is peace, then we may view again
With new-won eyes each other's truer form
And wonder. Grown more loving-kind and warm
We'll grasp firm hands and laugh at the old pain,
When it is peace. But until peace, the storm
he darkness and the thunder and the rain.

> C. H. Sorley

RECONCILIATION

When you are standing at your hero's grave,
Or near some homeless village where he died,
Remember, through your heart's rekindling pride,
The German soldiers who were loyal and brave.

Men fought like brutes; and hideous things were done,
And you have nourished hatred harsh and blind.
But in that Golgotha perhaps you'll find
The mothers of the men who killed your son.
November 1918

> Siegfried Sassoon

MAGPIES IN PICARDY

The magpies in Picardy
Are more than I can tell.
They flicker down the dusty roads
And cast a magic spell
On the men who march through Picardy,
Through Picardy to hell.

(The blackbird flies with panic,
The swallow goes with light,
The finches move like ladies,
The owl floats by at night;
But the great and flashing magpie
He flies as artists might.)

A magpie in Picardy
Told me secret things—
Of the music in white feathers,
And the sunlight that sings
And dances in deep shadows—
He told me with his wings.

(The hawk is cruel and rigid,
He watches from a height;
The rook is slow and sombre,
The robin loves to fight;
But the great and flashing magpie
He flies as lovers might.)

He told me that in Picardy,
An age ago or more,
While all his fathers still were eggs,
These dusty highways bore
Brown, singing soldiers marching out
Through Picardy to war.

He said that still through chaos
Works on the ancient plan,
And two things have altered not
Since first the world began—
The beauty of the wild green earth
And the bravery of man.

(For the sparrow flies unthinking
And quarrels in his flight;
The heron trails his legs behind,
The lark goes out of sight;
But the great and flashing magpie
He flies as poets might.)

T. P. Cameron Wilson

A THRUSH IN THE TRENCHES
(from *The Soldier*)

Suddenly he sang across the trenches,
   vivid in the fleeting hush
as a star-shell through the smashed black branches,
   a more than English thrush.

Suddenly he sang, and those who listened
   nor moved nor wondered, but
heard, all bewitched, the sweet unhastened
   crystal Magnificat.

One crouched, a muddied rifle clasping,
   and one a filled grenade,
but little cared they, while he went lisping
   the one clear tune he had.

Paused horror, hate and Hell a moment,
   (you could almost hear the sigh)
and still he sang to them, and so went
   (suddenly) singing by.

Humbert Wolfe

SPRING 1917

It is spring.
The buds break softly, silently.
This evening
The air is pink with the low sun,
And birds sing.

Do we believe
Men are now killing, dying—
This evening,
While the sky is pink with the low sun,
And birds sing?

No . . .
So they go on killing, dying,
This evening,
And through summer, autumn, winter,
And through spring.

Beatrice Mayor

IN FLANDERS FIELDS

In Flanders fields the poppies blow
Between the crosses, row on row,
   That mark our place; and in the sky
   The larks, still bravely singing, fly
Scarce heard amid the guns below.

We are the Dead. Short days ago
We lived, felt dawn, saw sunset glow,
   Loved and were loved, and now we lie
      In Flanders fields.

Take up our quarrel with the foe:
To you from failing hands we throw
   The torch; be yours to hold it high.
   If ye break faith with us who die
We shall not sleep, though poppies grow
   In Flanders fields.

    John McCrae

If I were the only girl in the world
And you were the only boy,
Nothing else would matter in the world today
We could go on loving in the same old way,
A garden of Eden made for two
With nothing to mar our joy,
I would say such wonderful things to you,
There would be such wonderful things to do,
If I were the only girl in the world,
And you were the only boy.

If you were the only Boche in the trench
And I had the only bomb,
Nothing else would matter in the world that day,
I would blow you up into eternity.
Chamber of Horrors, just made for two,
With nothing to spoil our fun;
There would be such a heap of things to do,
I should get your rifle and bayonet too,
If you were the only Boche in the trench,
And I had the only gun.

    Clifford Grey

51

THE WARD AT NIGHT

The rows of beds,
Each even spaced,
The blanket lying dark against the sheet,
The heavy breathing of the sick,
The fevered voices
Telling of the battle
At the front,
Of Home and Mother.

A quick, light step,
A white-capped figure
Silhouetted by the lantern's flame,
A needle, bearing sleep
And sweet forgetfulness.
A moan—
Then darkness, death.
God rest the valiant soul.

Anon

THE DEATH-BED

He drowsed and was aware of silence heaped
Round him, unshaken as the steadfast walls;
Aqueous like floating rays of amber light,
Soaring and quivering in the wings of sleep.
Silence and safety; and his mortal shore
Lipped by the inward, moonless waves of death.

Someone was holding water to his mouth.
He swallowed, unresisting; moaned and dropped
Through crimson gloom to darkness; and forgot
The opiate throb and ache that was his wound.
　Water—calm, sliding green above the weir.
　Water—a sky-lit alley for his boat,
　Bird-voiced, and bordered with reflected flowers
　And shaken hues of summer; drifting down,
　He dipped contented oars, and sighed, and slept.

Night, with a gust of wind, was in the ward,
Blowing the curtain to a glimmering curve.
Night. He was blind; he could not see the stars
Glinting among the wraiths of wandering cloud;
Queer blots of colour, purple, scarlet, green,
Flickered and faded in his drowning eyes.

Rain—he could hear it rustling through the dark;
Fragrance and passionless music woven as one;
Warm rain on drooping roses; pattering showers
That soak the woods; not the harsh rain that sweeps
Behind the thunder, but a trickling peace,
Gently and slowly washing life away.

He stirred, shifting his body; then the pain
Leapt like a prowling beast, and gripped and tore
His groping dreams with grinding claws and fangs.
   But someone was beside him; soon he lay
   Shuddering because that evil thing had passed.
   And death, who'd stepped toward him, paused and stared.

Light many lamps and gather round his bed.
Lend him your eyes, warm blood, and will to live.
Speak to him; rouse him; you may save him yet.
He's young; he hated War; how should he die
When cruel old campaigners win safe through?

But death replied: 'I choose him.' So he went,
And there was silence in the summer night;
Silence and safety; and the veils of sleep.
Then, far away, the thudding of the guns.

Siegfried Sassoon

CONSCIOUS

His fingers wake, and flutter; up the bed.
His eyes come open with a pull of will,
Helped by the yellow may-flowers by his head.
The blind-cord drawls across the window-sill . . .
What a smooth floor the ward has! What a rug!
Who is that talking somewhere out of sight?
Why are they laughing? What's inside that jug?
'Nurse! Doctor!'—'Yes; all right, all right.'

But sudden evening muddles all the air—
There seems no time to want a drink of water,
Nurse looks so far away. And here and there
Music and roses burst through crimson slaughter.
He can't remember where he saw blue sky.
More blankets. Cold. He's cold. And yet so hot.
And there's no light to see the voices by;
There is no time to ask—he knows not what.

Wilfred Owen

HERE DEAD LIE WE

Here dead lie we because we did not choose
    To live and shame the land from which we sprung.
Life, to be sure, is nothing much to lose;
    But young men think it is, and we were young.

A. E. Housman

IN MEMORIAM
(*Easter, 1915*)

The flowers left thick at nightfall in the wood
This Eastertide call into mind the men,
Now far from home, who, with their sweethearts, should
Have gathered them and will do never again.

Edward Thomas

EASTER MONDAY
(*In Memoriam Edward Thomas*)

In the last letter that I had from France
You thanked me for the silver Easter egg
Which I had hidden in the box of apples
You liked to munch beyond all other fruit.
You found the egg the Monday before Easter,
And said, 'I will praise Easter Monday now—
It was such a lovely morning'. Then you spoke
Of the coming battle and said, 'This is the eve.
Good-bye. And may I have a letter soon.'

That Easter Monday was a day for praise,
It was such a lovely morning. In our garden
We sowed our earliest seeds, and in the orchard
The apple-bud was ripe. It was the eve.
There are three letters that you will not get.

Eleanor Farjeon

PREAEMATURI

When men are old, and their friends die,
They are not so sad,
Because their love is running slow,
And cannot spring from the wound with so sharp a pain;
And they are happy with many memories,
And only a little while to be alone.

But we are young, and our friends are dead
Suddenly, and our quick love is torn in two;
So our memories are only hopes that came to nothing.
We are left alone like old men; we should be dead
—But there are years and years in which we shall still be young.

Margaret Postgate Cole

FUTILITY

Move him into the sun—
Gently its touch awoke him once,
At home, whispering of fields unsown.
Always it woke him, even in France,
Until this morning and this snow.
If anything might rouse him now
The kind old sun will know.

Think how it wakes the seeds,—
Woke, once, the clays of a cold star.
Are limbs, so dear-achieved, are sides,
Full-nerved—still warm—too hard to stir?
Was it for this the clay grew tall?
—O what made fatuous sunbeams toil
To break earth's sleep at all?

Wilfred Owen

PERHAPS—
(To R.A.L. Died of Wounds in France, 23rd December, 1915)

Perhaps some day the sun will shine again,
   And I shall see that still the skies are blue,
And feel once more I do not live in vain,
   Although bereft of You.

Perhaps the golden meadows at my feet
   Will make the sunny hours of Spring seem gay,
And I shall find the white May blossoms sweet,
   Though You have passed away.

Perhaps the summer woods will shimmer bright,
   And crimson roses once again be fair,
And autumn harvest fields a rich delight,
   Although You are not there.

Perhaps some day I shall not shrink in pain
   To see the passing of the dying year,
And listen to the Christmas songs again,
   Although You cannot hear.

But, though kind Time may many joys renew,
   There is one greatest joy I shall not know
Again, because my heart for loss of You
   Was broken, long ago.

Vera Brittain

from FOR THE FALLEN
(September 1914)

They went with songs to the battle, they were young,
Straight of limb, true of eye, steady and aglow.
They were staunch to the end against odds uncounted,
They fell with their faces to the foe.

They shall grow not old, as we that are left grow old:
Age shall not weary them, nor the years condemn.
At the going down of the sun and in the morning
We will remember them.

Laurence Binyon

OBE

I know a Captain of Industry,
Who made big bombs for the RFC,
And collared a lot of £ s. d.—
And he—thank God!—has the OBE.

I know a Lady of Pedigree,
Who asked some soldiers out to tea,
And said 'Dear me!' and 'Yes, I see'—
And she—thank God!—has the OBE.

I know a fellow of twenty-three,
Who got a job with a fat MP—
(Not caring much for the Infantry.)
And he—thank God!—has the OBE.

I had a friend; a friend, and he
Just held the line for you and me,
And kept the Germans from the sea,
And died—without the OBE.
     Thank God!
He died without the OBE.

A. A. Milne

THE LAMENT OF THE DEMOBILIZED

'Four years,' some say consolingly. 'Oh well,
What's that? You're young. And then it must have been
A very fine experience for you!'
And they forget
How others stayed behind and just got on—
Got on the better since we were away.
And we came home and found
They had achieved, and men revered their names,
But never mentioned ours;
And no one talked heroics now, and we
Must just go back and start again once more.
'You threw four years into the melting-pot—
Did you indeed!' these others cry. 'Oh well,
The more fool you!'
And we're beginning to agree with them.

Vera Brittain

DOES IT MATTER?

Does it matter?—losing your legs? . . .
For people will always be kind,
And you need not show that you mind
When the others come in after hunting
To gobble their muffins and eggs.

Does it matter?—losing your sight? . . .
There's such splendid work for the blind;
And people will always be kind,
As you sit on the terrace remembering
And turning your face to the light.

Do they matter?—those dreams from the pit? . . .
You can drink and forget and be glad,
And people won't say that you're mad;
For they'll know that you've fought for your country
And no one will worry a bit.

Siegfried Sassoon

BACK

They ask me where I've been,
And what I've done and seen.
But what can I reply
Who know it wasn't I,
But some one just like me,
Who went across the sea
And with my head and hands
Killed men in foreign lands . . .
Though I must bear the blame,
Because he bore my name.

Wilfrid Gibson

A STORY OF TODAY

An open drawer, a woman lowly kneeling,
Some little crimson shoes, a lock of hair,
Some childish toys, an engine and a trumpet,
A headless horse, a battered Teddy bear.
Some school-boy books, all inky, torn and thumb-marked,
A treasured bat, his favourite cricket ball,
The things he loved, the letters that he wrote her—
And now she places on the top of all
A soldier's sword, his photograph, in khaki—
The boyish eyes smile back into her eyes,
While in her hand she holds a V.C. tightly,
And in her heart a grave in Flanders lies.

Constance Powell

VILLAGE CRICKET

A lush green field. Upon a shaven patch,
Stolen from daisies and buttercups was played
The Saturday match.
Sudden, a lusty shout—
'Well caught, Bill!' from the opposing side,
And necks were craned if it might be described
Which stranger made the catch
That got our best man out.
'Oo was it?' . . . 'Wot's 'is name?'—
'Is THAT 'im over there?' . . . 'Poor chap, e's lame—
Bit of the war touch.'

In Flanders fields they lie so still, so quiet,
No sound,
Even of bat and ball,
Disturbs their rest at all.
And yet, dear flannelled ghosts, they seemed to gather
Beside the cripple on the cricket ground,
And, noiseless, clap their hands,
Happy that still, in this their land of lands,
The others play
The summer game in fields on Saturday.

Teresa Hooley

AFTERMATH

Have you forgotten yet? . . .
For the world's events have rumbled on since those gagged days,
Like traffic checked while at the crossing of city-ways:
And the haunted gap in your mind has filled with thoughts that
   flow
Like clouds in the lit heaven of life; and you're a man reprieved to
   go,
Taking your peaceful share of Time, with joy to spare.
But the past is just the same—and War's a bloody game . . .
Have you forgotten yet? . . .
Look down, and swear by the slain of the War that you'll never
   forget.

Do you remember the dark months you held the sector at Mametz?
The nights you watched and wired and dug and piled sandbags on
   parapets?
Do you remember the rats; and the stench
Of corpses rotting in front of the front-line trench—
And dawn coming, dirty-white, and chill with a hopeless rain?
Do you ever stop and ask, 'Is it all going to happen again?'

Do you remember that hour of din before the attack—
And the anger, the blind compassion that seized and shook you

As you peered at the doomed and haggard faces of your men?
Do you remember the stretcher-cases lurching back
With dying eyes and lolling heads—those ashen-grey
Masks of the lads who once were keen and kind and gay?

Have you forgotten yet? . . .
Look up, and swear by the green of the spring that you'll never
   forget.

   Siegfried Sassoon

THE
SECOND WORLD WAR

from AUTUMN JOURNAL

Today was a beautiful day, the sky was a brilliant
  Blue for the first time for weeks and weeks
But posters flapping on the railings tell the flustered
  World that Hitler speaks, that Hitler speaks
And we cannot take it in and we go to our daily
  Jobs to the dull refrain of the caption 'War'
Buzzing around us as from hidden insects
  And we think 'This must be wrong, it has happened before,
Just like this before, we must be dreaming' . . .
And a train begins to chug and I wonder what the morning
  Paper will say
And decide to go quickly to sleep for the morning already
  Is with us, the day is to-day.

Louis MacNeice

BOURNEMOUTH, SEPTEMBER 3rd, 1939

My summer ends, and term begins next week.
Why am I here in Bournemouth, with my aunt
And 'Uncle Bill', who something tells me can't
Be really my uncle? People speak
In hushed, excited tones. Down on the beach
An aeroplane comes in low over the sea
And there's a scattering as people reach
For towels and picnic gear and books, and flee
Towards the esplanade. Back at the hotel
We hear what the Prime Minister has said.
'So it's begun.' 'Yes, it was bound to.' 'Well,
Give it till Christmas.' Later, tucked in bed,
I hear the safe sea roll and wipe away
The castles I had built in sand that day.

Anthony Thwaite

THE SECOND WORLD WAR

The voice said 'We are at War'
And I was afraid, for I did not know what this meant.
My sister and I ran to our friends next door
As if they could help. History was lessons learnt
      With ancient dates, but here

Was something utterly new,
The radio, called the wireless then, had said
That the country would have to be brave. There was much to do.
And I remember that night as I lay in bed
      I thought of soldiers who

Had stood on our nursery floor
Holding guns, on guard and stiff. But war meant blood
Shed over battle-fields, Cavalry galloping. War
On that September Sunday made us feel frightened
      Of what our world waited for.

Elizabeth Jennings

from AUTOBIOGRAPHY

Carrying my gas-mask to school every day
buying saving stamps
remembering my National Registration Number
(ZMGM/136/3 see I can still remember it)
avoiding Careless Talk Digging for Victory
looking for German spies everywhere
Oh yes, I did my bit for my country that long dark winter,
me and Winston and one or two others,
wearing my tin hat whenever possible
Singing 'Hang out the Washing on the Siegfried Line'
aircraft-recognition charts pinned to my bedroom wall
the smell of paint on toy soldiers
doing paintings of Spitfires and Hurricanes,
              Lancasters and Halifaxes
along with a Heinkel or a Messerschmitt plunging
          helplessly into the sea in the background

pink light in the sky from Liverpool burning fifty miles away
the thunder of daylight flying fortresses high overhead
                         shaking the elderberry tree
bright barrage-balloons flying over the docks
morning curve of the bay seen from the park on the hill
after coming out of the air-raid shelter
listening for the 'All Clear' siren
listening to Vera Lynn Dorothy Lamour Allan Jones and the
   Andrews Sisters
clutching my father's hand tripping over the unfamiliar kerb
I walk over every day
in the black-out.

Adrian Henri

EMPTY YOUR POCKETS

Empty your pockets, Tom, Dick and Harry,
Strip your identity, leave it behind.
Lawyer, garage-hand, grocer, don't tarry
With your own country, your own kind.

Leave all your letters. Suburb and township,
Green fen and grocery, slip-way and bay,
Hot-spring and prairie, smoke stack and coal-tip,
Leave in our keeping while you're away.

Tom, Dick, and Harry, plain names and numbers,
Pilot, observer and gunner depart.
Their personal litter only encumbers
Somebody's head, somebody's heart.

John Pudney

A WAR

There set out, slowly, for a Different World,
At four, on winter mornings, different legs . . .
You can't break eggs without making an omelette
—That's what they tell the eggs.

Randall Jarrell

*I never raised my boy
    to be a soldier
I brought him up to be
    my pride and joy.
Who dares to lay a gun
    upon his shoulder,
And teach him how to kill
    another mother's boy.
I never raised my boy
    to be a soldier.
I brought him up to stay
    at home with me.
There would be no war to-day,
    if every mother would say
I never raised my boy
    to be a soldier.*

Traditional North Country

from SONG FOR A SOLDIER

I march along and march along and ask myself each day:
If I should go and lose the war, then what will Mother say?
The Sergeant will be cross and red, the Captain cross and pink,
But all I ever ask myself is, What will Mother think?

   For
   I
   Kissed her at the kitchen door,
   And promised her as sure as sure
   I'd win the what-d'you-call-it war—
      'You wait,' I said to Mother.
   She said, 'You mean you'll win the war?'
   I said, 'By next September sure—
   Why, that's what I'm enlisting for,'
      I told my dear old Mother.

I march along and march along and hardly dare to speak
For planning how to finish off the war by Monday week;
For Mother and the Sergeant will be very cross and hot
If we should lose the war because of something I've forgot.

   Yes,
   I
   Kissed him at the cook-house door,
   And promised him I'd win the war—
   'Why, that's what I've enlisted for,'
      I told my dear old Sergeant.
   He said, 'You'll *win* the ruddy war?'
   I said, 'Oh, Sergeant, keep it pure,
   Of course I'll win the nasty war—
      And then I'll be a Sergeant.'

   A. A. Milne

TELL US THE TRICKS

Say, soldier! Tell us the tricks,
   the tackle of your trade;
The passage of your hours;
   the plans that you have made—
Of what do you think—what consider?
Tell us of the slow process,
That gradual change
   from man to soldier—?

And what can I say, what reply?
   There is no answer.
The tale is hidden in the eye.
The soldier's here—the man is not:
Man's voice was lost;
The sex decayed
By the bitter bayonet—the chattering shot
The growth delayed.
The brief days of youth,
And its forgotten past,
Cannot be commanded to appear,
We hope they may at last
   —some other time—some different year.

Paul Scott

Private Jones came in one night,
Full of cheer and very bright,
He'd been out all day upon a spree.
He bumped into Sergeant Smeck,
Put his arms around his neck,
And in his ear he whispered tenderly:
Kiss me Goodnight, Sergeant-Major,
Tuck me in my little wooden bed.
We all love you, Sergeant-Major,
When we hear you bawling 'Show a leg!'
Don't forget to wake me in the morning,
And bring me round a nice hot cup of tea,
Kiss me Goodnight, Sergeant-Major,
Sergeant-Major, be a Mother to me!

from LESSONS OF THE WAR (to Alan Michell)

Vixi duellis nuper idoneus
Et militavi non sine gloria

I—Naming of Parts

Today we have naming of parts. Yesterday,
We had daily cleaning. And to-morrow morning,
We shall have what to do after firing. But today,
Today we have naming of parts. Japonica
Glistens like coral in all of the neighbouring gardens
  And today we have naming of parts.

This is the lower sling swivel. And this
Is the upper sling swivel, whose use you will see
When you are given your slings. And this is the piling swivel,
Which in your case you have not got. The branches
Hold in the gardens their silent, eloquent gestures,
  Which in our case we have not got.

This is the safety-catch, which is always released
With an easy flick of the thumb. And please do not let me
See anyone using his finger. You can do it quite easy
If you have any strength in your thumb. The blossoms
Are fragile and motionless, never letting anyone see
     Any of them using their finger.

And this you can see is the bolt. The purpose of this
Is to open the breech, as you see. We can slide it
Rapidly backwards and forwards; we call this
Easing the spring. And rapidly backwards and forwards
The early bees are assaulting and fumbling the flowers:
     They call it easing the Spring.

They call it easing the Spring; it is perfectly easy
If you have any strength in your thumb: like the bolt,
And the breech, and the cocking-piece, and the point of balance,
Which in our case we have not got; and the almond-blossom
Silent in all of the gardens and the bees going backwards and
     forwards,
     For today we have naming of parts.

Henry Reed

POEM

The pale wild roses star the banks of green
and poignant poppies startle their fields with red,
while peace like sunlight rests on the summer scene,
though lilac that flashed in hedges is dulled and dead:
in the faint sky the singing birds go over,
the sheep are quiet where the quiet grasses are.
I go to the plane among the peaceful clover,
but climbing in the Hampden, shut myself in war.

Herbert Corby

71

AEROPLANES

A dragonfly
in a flecked grey sky.

Its silvered planes
break the wide and still
harmony of space.

Around it shells
flash
their fumes
burgeoning to blooms
smoke-lilies that float
along the sky.

Among them darts
a dragonfly.

Herbert Read

PARACHUTE DESCENT

Snap back the canopy,
Pull out the oxygen tube,
Flick the harness pin
And slap out into the air
Clear of the machine.

Did you ever dream when you were young
Of floating through the air, hung
Between the clouds and the gay
Be-blossomed land?
Did you ever stand and say,
'To sit and think and be alone
In the middle of the sky
Is my one most perfect wish'?

That was a fore-knowing;
You knew that some day
To satiate an inward crave
You must play with the wave
Of a cloud. And shout aloud
In the clean air,
The untouched-by-worldly-things-and-mean air,
With exhilarated living.

You knew that you must float
From the sun above the clouds
To the gloom beneath, from a world
Of rarefied splendour to one
Of cheapened dirt, close-knit
In its effort to encompass man
In death.

So you can stay in the clouds, boy,
You can let your soul go onwards,
You have no ties on earth,
You could never have accomplished
Anything. Your ideas and ideals
Were too high. So you can stay
In the sky, boy, and have no fear.

David Bourne

THE CHILDREN'S PARTY

Quick as shuttles the children move
  Through the lighted room,
Where flowers glow in the scented air
  And candles bloom;
Their voices are fresh as a field of larks
  Over springing wheat;
They weave the web of what is to come
  With their dancing feet.

Like eager ponies snuffing the grass
  And the south-west weather,
Tossing their heads and lifting their feet
  They run together.
By the purring fire on his nurse's knee
  The youngest one
Stretches his toes and his tiny hands
  To catch the fun.

Out in the night, over the snow,
Grimly the dark gun-carriages go,
  Where are they bound for?
    No one knows,
But the curtain shakes,
  Oh, draw it close!

    Eiluned Lewis

BLACK-OUT

Night comes now
Without the artistry of hesitation, the surprising
Last minute turn-aside into a modulation,
Without the rising
Final assertion of promise before the fall.

Darkness now
Comes by routine of cardboard shutter, rattle of curtain,
Comes like a sentence everyone's learnt to utter,
Undoubted and certain,
Too stupid to interest anyone at all.

Valentine Ackland

I'VE FINISHED MY BLACK-OUT
(*The Song of a Triumphant Housewife*)

I've finished my Black-out!
   There's paint on the carpet and glue on my hair
   There's a saw in the bathroom and spills on the stair,
   And a drawing pin lost in the seat of a chair,
     But I've finished my Black-out.

The bedrooms are draped with funereal black
Except for the little one facing the back,
And that we have had to nail up with a sack,
     But I've finished my Black-out!

    Oh, I've finished my Black-out!
Policemen and wardens may peer and may pry,
And enemy planes may look down from the sky,
But they won't see a pin-prick however they try,
     For I've finished my Black-out!

Anon

75

When Billy Brown goes out at night
He wears or carries something white
When Mrs Brown is in the black-out
She likes to wear her old white mac out.
And Sally Brown straps round her shoulder
A natty plain white knick-knack holder
The reason why they wear this white
Is so they may be seen at night.

Billy Brown's Own Highway Code
For black-outs is 'Stay off the Road'.
He'll never step out and begin
To meet a bus that's pulling in.
He doesn't wave his torch at night
But flags his bus with something white
He never jostles in a queue
But waits and takes his turn—Do you?

OCTOBER 1940

When leaves like guineas start to fall
And sycamore and elm begin
Red tears to shed, then Autumn's in
And Summer gone beyond recall.

Thick, thick they fell from London trees
In years that seem an age ago;
They cantered then down Rotten Row
And ran down Broad Walk with the breeze.

The children laughed to see them run
And caught them in their merry flight
And we were glad, for their delight
Beneath the thin October sun.

But there's another fall today,
When bombs instead of leaves come down
To drive our children out of town
And us to ground. We will repay.

Anon

The Blackout

Why not wear something white instead?

EVACUEE

The slum had been his home since he was born;
And then war came, and he was rudely torn
From all he'd ever known; and with his case
Of mean necessities, brought to a place
Of silences and space; just boom of sea
And sough of wind; small wonder then that he
Crept out one night to seek his sordid slum,
And thought to find his way. By dawn he'd come
A few short miles; and cattle in their herds
Gazed limpidly as he trudged by, and birds
Just stirring in first light, awoke to hear
His lonely sobbing, born of abject fear
Of sea and hills and sky; of silent night
Unbroken by the sound of shout and fight.

Edith Pickthall

ALBERT EVACUATED

Have you heard how young Albert Ramsbottom
Was evacuated from home
With his mother, clean socks and a toothbrush,
Some Syrup of Figs and a comb.

The stick with the 'orse's 'ead 'andle,
They decided that they'd leave behind
To keep safe with the things they weren't wanting,
Like their gasmasks, and things of that kind.

Pa saw them off at the station,
And shed a few crocodile's tears
As he waved them goodbye from the platform—
T'was the best break he'd had in ten years.

Ma got corner seat for young Albert,
Who amused all the rest of the team
By breathing hot breaths on the window,
And writing some swear words in steam.

They arrived at last somewhere in England,
And straight to their billet were shown;
There was one room for mother
But Albert was in a small room of his own.

The very first night in the black-out,
Young Albert performed quite a feat
By hanging head first from the window,
And shining his torch down the street.

It flashed on an A.R.P. Warden
Patrolling with leisurely gait;
'Good Heavens,' said he, 'it's Tarzan,
I'd better go investigate.'

So reading his book of instructions
To make himself doubly sure,
Then in an official manner
Proceeded to knock on the door.

It was opened by Mrs Ramsbottom
'Now then,' said she, 'what's to do?'
And in stern air-warden manner, he said
'I'm going to interrogate you.'

This fair upset Mrs Ramsbottom,
Her face was a picture to see;
'I'll have you know you'll do nowt of the sort,
I'm a respectable woman,' said she.

'Has your son been evacuated?'
Said the A.R.P. man at the door.
'He'd all them things done as a baby,' said Mother
'He's not being done any more.

'Be off, now,' said Mrs Ramsbottom
As she bustled him out of the porch;
And the A.R.P. man patted Albert,
And then confiscated his torch.

Now that were unlucky for Albert,
He had no torch to see him to bed;
But being a bright little fellow
He switched on the hall light instead.

'Put out that light,' a voice shouted.
'Where's the men of our A.R.P.?'
'I've told them already,' the warden replied,
'They take no bloody notice of me.'

Soon Mrs Ramsbottom and Albert
Were feeling quite homesick and sad;
So they thanked the landlady most kindly,
And prepared to go back home to Dad.

When at last they reached home to Father
They were fed up and had quite enough;
But in the front parlour they found six young women,
And Father were doing his stuff.

'Hello, Mother,' said Mr Ramsbottom,
'Come right on in, don't be afraid,
When you went away I joined Ambulance Corps—
I'm instructing the girls in first aid.'

'First aid,' said Mrs Ramsbottom
With a horrible look on her brow.
'If ever you wanted first aid in your life,
By gum, you'll be wanting it now.'

Stanley Holloway

THE SENTRY

I have begun to die.
For now at last I know
That there is no escape
From Night. Not any dream
Nor breathless images of sleep
Touch my bat's-eyes. I hang
Leathery-arid from the hidden roof
Of Night, and sleeplessly
I watch within Sleep's province.
I have left
The lovely bodies of the boy and girl
Deep in each other's placid arms;
And I have left
The beautiful lanes of sleep
That barefoot lovers follow to this last
Cold shore of thought I guard.
I have begun to die
And the guns' implacable silence
Is my black interim, my youth and age,
In the flower of fury, the folded poppy,
Night.

Alun Lewis

FLEET FIGHTER

'Good show!' he said, leaned his head back and laughed.
'They're wizard types!' he said, and held his beer
Steadily, looked at it and gulped it down
Out of its jam-jar, took a cigarette
And blew a neat smoke ring into the air.
'After this morning's prang I've got the twitch;
I thought I'd had it in that teased-out kite.'
His eyes were blue, and older than his face,
His single stripe had known a lonely war
But all his talk and movements showed his age.
His whole life was the air and his machine,
He had no thought but of the latest 'mod',
His jargon was of aircraft or of beer.
'And what will you do afterwards?' I said,
Then saw his puzzled face, and caught my breath.
There was no afterwards for him, but death.

Olivia FitzRoy

WAR POET

I am the man who looked for peace and found
My own eyes barbed.
I am the man who groped for words and found
An arrow in my hand.
I am the builder whose firm walls surround
A slipping land.
When I grow sick or mad
Mock me not nor chain me:
When I reach for the wind
Cast me not down:
Though my face is a burnt book
And a wasted town.

Sidney Keyes

SIMPLIFY ME WHEN I'M DEAD

Remember me when I am dead
and simplify me when I'm dead.

As the processes of earth
strip off the colour and the skin
take the brown hair and blue eye

and leave me simpler than at birth,
when hairless I came howling in
as the moon came in the cold sky.

Of my skeleton perhaps
so stripped, a learned man will say
'He was of such a type and intelligence,' no more.

Thus when in a year collapse
particular memories, you may
deduce, from the long pain I bore

the opinions I held, who was my foe
and what I left, even my appearance
but incidents will be no guide.

Time's wrong-way telescope will show
a minute man ten years hence
and by distance simplified.

Through that lens see if I seem
substance or nothing: of the world
deserving mention or charitable oblivion

not by momentary spleen
or love into decision hurled,
leisurely arrive at an opinion.

Remember me when I am dead
and simplify me when I'm dead.

Keith Douglas

THE CHILD

How can I teach, how can I save,
This child whose features are my own,
Whose feet run down the ways where I have walked?

How can I name that vision past the corner,
How warn the seed that grows to constant anger,
How can I draw the map that tells no lies?

His world is a small world of hours and minutes,
Hedgerows shut in the horizons of his thought,
His loves are uncritical and deep,
His anger innocent and sudden like a minnow.

His eyes, acute and quick, are unprotected,
Unsandalled still, his feet run down the lane,
Down to that lingering horror in the brambles,
The limp crashed airman, in the splintered goggles.

Michael Roberts

THE BULL

Into the paddock from his parachute
The alien airman dropped and, still half-dazed,
He failed to notice the old bull that grazed
A dozen yards away, until the brute,
Startled to anger by such insolence,
With frothing muzzle lifted suddenly
Let out a bellow and, crashing through the fence
Charged head-down at his country's enemy.

Wilfrid Gibson

SONG OF THE DYING GUNNER

Oh mother my mouth is full of stars
As cartridges in the tray
My blood is a twin-branched scarlet tree
And it runs all runs away.

Oh Cooks to the Galley is sounded off
And the lads are down in the mess
But I lie done by the forrard gun
With a bullet in my breast.

Don't send me a parcel at Christmas time
Of socks and nutty and wine
And don't depend on a long weekend
By the Great Western Railway line.

Farewell, Aggie Weston, the Barracks at Guz,
Hang my tiddley suit on the door
I'm sewn up neat in a canvas sheet
And I shan't be home no more.

Charles Causley

FOR JOHNNY

Do not despair
For Johnny-Head-in-Air;
He sleeps as sound
As Johnny-underground.

Fetch out no shroud
For Johnny-in-the-Cloud,
And keep your tears
For him in after years.

Better by far
For Johnny-the-bright-star
To keep your head
And see his children fed.

John Pudney

FOR THIS RELIEF

Because your husband was killed in a concentration camp,
Because your brother was beaten until he died,
Because your friends have been taken away and tortured,
Because you have lost all faith, all hope, all desire,
Because there is nothing more in the whole wide world for you to
    lose,
I, full of compassion, send for your comfort,
Two of my husband's vests and a pair of old tennis shoes.

Virginia Graham

PIGTAIL

When all the women in the transport
had their heads shaved
four workmen with brooms made of birch twigs
swept up
and gathered up the hair

Behind clean glass
the stiff hair lies
of those suffocated in gas chambers
there are pins and side combs
in this hair

The hair is not shot through with light
is not parted by the breeze
is not touched by any hand
or rain or lips

In huge chests
clouds of dry hair
of those suffocated
and a faded plait
a pigtail with a ribbon
pulled at school
by naughty boys.

The Museum, Auschwitz, 1948

Tadeusz Różewicz
Trans. Adam Czerniawski

MASSACRE OF THE BOYS

The children cried 'Mummy!
But I have been good!
It's dark in here! Dark!'

See them They are going to the bottom
See the small feet
they went to the bottom Do you see
that print
of a small foot here and there

pockets bulging
with string and stones
and little horses made of wire

A great closed plain
like a figure of geometry
and a tree of black smoke
a vertical
dead tree
with no star in its crown

The Museum, Auschwitz, 1948

Tadeusz Różewicz
Trans. Adam Czerniawski

ATTIC

We stored some dusty things up there.
It smelt of mothballs and bare wood,
A spaceless jumble place to hide.
All day we crouched below the sun
Too young to feel the utter fear.
We heard them scream and beat with sticks—
Now they were near—

               a widow's world
Crashed through her glass, old limbless
Porcelain and brass, her table
Torn from her late, careful touching.
We trembled.—

            Someone shouted: 'Halt,
Der Führer will das Treiben nicht!'
And all was quiet.—

              Then my mother
Cooked some food, and we were waiting
For my father's earth-worn footfall
Returning from the darkening trees.

Lotte Kramer

from ALL-CLEAR

Miss Ryder is showing us how to breathe.
Eighteen of us, at triple desks,
in Mickey Mouse gas-masks,
sad as cages,
mine smelling of my brother's rubber sheet,
my mother's still-warm shoes.
And in the yard, at playtime,
each mouse-face stretched to sorrow
at the top of every swing,
Ken Dykes and Chippy Fletcher
slug it out,
crying quietly,
unable to let go,
taking turns—impeccably—to strike.

'Underneath the spreading chestnut tree,
Mr Churchill said to me,
"If you want your gas-masks free
join the blinking A.R.P."'

We loose our hands and scatter
to the far points of the yard,
and Ernest Moon, as always,
squats behind a dinner-churn,
jersey pulled over his head.

The oil-lamp stutters in our air-raid shelter,
my father's massive shadow
enriching the dried roots of the sods above.
Mr Sutton blacks his face
with cork charred by the candle,
cleans the barrel of his rifle
with a plug of cotton wool.
'If Hitler lands at Frodsham
we'll trim his moustache at Barber Stalker's',
he whispers through his emphysema.
I strain against the ventilation slit:
smoke subdues the sky, in patches,
something large
is rattling down the side of Frodsham Hill,
and the warning siren
halts the blurp of tugs on the canal.

My mother is ironing scraps of silver paper
we've saved for the wounded soldiers.
To patch their bullet-holes?
To make neat chimneys
for the smoke inside their bones
to flow more easily away?
To manufacture artificial limbs?
Mr Rigby hides his limp,
but when he leapt across the daffodils
to catch my green balloon
his left leg glinted in the sun.

The bomb crater, up Gasworks Lane,
is disappointing,
cold, dry, no sign of blood,
no face-shapes blasted in the sand.
Too shallow, even, for the patient cow
who died last week
in Mr Maddock's field
—sad, stiff-tailed,
mourned by quiet flies.

Traitorous for handling
these shrapnel shards we swap at school,
their colour greasy to the touch,
we inspect our hands for warts
or grey stigmata.

Who are these enemies with silly names,
beyond our tiptoed vision
even from the top of Frodsham Hill,
shapes tangled
in the wireless hiss and crackle,
when my father spins the yellow knob?
'That Mr Hitler. He's a fidget.',
said Miss Helsby
when the firemen pulled her out.

Miss Ryder dips her ladle in the barrel,
tips chocolate powder
from our friends across the sea
into our tins and jars,
paper bags when these are full.
On Hillfields, after school,
behind our snail-race track,
we sniff it, tongue it, gulp it down,
wonder if we'll ever breathe again.
Next week we give Ernest Moon
—who'd missed the gift through croup—
a jar of sand from Crowton quarry:
and we snort, bite knuckles,
as he slowly eats it, puzzled.

'Oh Mr Churchill, what shall I do?
My cap blew off on Windy Rock
And floated down the brew.'

John Latham

The glass jars in the sweet shops
  Once packed with sheer delight,
Stand often now quite empty,
  A sad and sorry sight;
They'd butterscotch—they'd bull's-eyes,
  All sorts of sugared bliss—
But now the times have changed a bit,
  And nothing comes amiss!
A common vegetable behold!
  Is handed as a sweetmeat—cold—
    So carrots may be seen in shops
    Once sacred to pure lollipops!

DRAWING A BANANA
(A Memory of Childhood during the War)

Forty of us looked longingly at the yellow finger
Plumped, curved, bearing strange black marks.
The word 'banana' purred insistently round the classroom.
Our teacher, furrowed by severity as much as age,
Smiled slightly, then mounted her trophy on a box for us
To draw with thick pencil on thin, grey page.

We licked our lips in hope. Dimly we thought
The banana would be shared, perhaps that it would stretch
Like the bread and fish once did among the multitude.
A clearer idea flowered: it was for one child to win.
The bloom was nipped as it emerged our teacher meant to keep
The prize herself, and all alone to strip its golden skin.

It was boring drawing that banana. My leaden lines
Smudged with rubbings out didn't resemble the fruit taunting
My hungry eyes. I couldn't quite remember seeing
A 'live' banana before—there was a war to fight
And grown-ups said we had to go without and make do.
Yet if I closed my eyes I could conjure up a feast of a sight:

A window of violet-iced cakes and chocolates heaped
On silver trays belonging to a piece of magic time.
As far as my certainty stretched back war enveloped all.
War meant sombre ships sliding slowly down the Clyde,
Sirens, snuggling with cocoa in the cupboard beneath the stairs
Though the only bomb that fell was on the moors and no one died.

Fear couldn't touch me for I knew with crystal-cut clarity
Our side was in the right and therefore bound to win.
Yet my parents frowned and talked in hushed gloom
By the crackling wireless. If the Germans march through France,
Never mind, I urged. With God fighting for England
It was in the fields of Hell that the fiend Hitler would dance.

I was proved right in the end, but long before then
My belief was crumbling in that lost paradise, peace.
I dreamed, daydreamed the war had ended. Warships
Decked out in scarlet streamers docked at our little pier,
Soldiers surged down the gangways to crowds in gaudy clothes,
Music reeled from radios—there'd be no more news to hear.

Ice-cream parlours would grow pink and come alive
To sell real ices not those fadings on the walls.
Rationing would end—I'd buy chocolate drops in mounds.
Bulging hands of bananas would hang in the greengrocer's shop
But instead of drawing stupidly I'd bite into a bunch
And no grim-faced grown-up would shout at me to stop.

Myra Schneider

SHELLS

All day like an automaton
She fits the shells into the gauge,
Hour after hour, to earn the wage
To keep her and her little son:
All day, hour after hour, she stands
Handling cold death with calloused hands.

She dare not think, she dare not feel
What happens to the shells that she
Handles and checks so carefully,
Or what, within each case of steel
Is packed as, hour by hour she stands
Handling cold death with calloused hands.

Wilfrid Gibson

*She's the girl that makes the thing
That drills the hole, that holds the spring
That drives the rod, that turns the knob
That works the thingummybob.
It's a ticklish sort of job
Making a thing for a thingummybob
Especially when you don't know what it's for.
And it's the girl that makes the thing
That holds the oil that oils the ring
That makes the thingummy bob that's going to win the war. . . .*

SONG OF THE BOMBER

I am purely evil;
Hear the thrum
Of my evil engine;
Evilly I come.

> The stars are thick as flowers
> In the meadows of July;
> A fine night for murder
> Winging through the sky.
>
> Bombs shall be the bounty
> Of the lovely night;
> Death the desecration
> Of the fields of light.

I am purely evil,
Come to destroy
Beauty and goodness,
Tenderness and joy.

Ethel Mannin

TO A BARRAGE BALLOON

We used to say 'If pigs could fly!'
    And now they do.
I saw one sailing in the sky
Some thousand feet above his sty,
    A fat one, too!
I scarcely could believe my eyes,
So just imagine my surprise
To see so corpulent a pig
Inconsequently dance a jig
    Upon a cloud.
And, when elated by the show
I clapped my hands and called 'Bravo!'
    He turned and bowed.
Then, all at once, he seemed to flop
And dived behind a chimney-top
    Out of my sight.
'He's down' thought I; but not at all,
'Twas only pride that had the fall:
    To my delight
He rose, quite gay and debonair,
Resolved to go on dancing there
    Both day and night.

    So pigs can fly,
    They really do,
This chap, though anchored in the slime,
Could reach an altitude sublime—
    A pig, 'tis true!
    I wish I knew
Just how not only pigs but men
Might rise to nobler heights again
    Right in the blue
    And start anew!

May Morton

LADYBIRD, LADYBIRD

'Ladybird, ladybird,
fly away home . . .'
leopard-winged ladybirds,
why do they roam?
the children were singing the summer refrain,
'Ladybird, ladybird,
fly home again!'

Outside, a tired woman
lingered to say,
'You wouldn't know of
a place I could stay . . . ?'
Weary, with bundles—
life had gone west.
'Bombed out last night, dear—
I—just need a rest.'

(Children and ladybirds
singing of flight . . .)
'I had two kiddies, dear—
until last night . . .'
Oh, ladybird, ladybird—
So it goes on—
YOUR HOUSE IS AFIRE
AND YOUR CHILDREN ARE GONE

Ruth Tomalin

ST. PAUL'S CATHEDRAL

In the event of an

AIR RAID

the Crypt will be open to the Public

LOSING FACE

This is my doodle-bug face. Do you like it?
  It's supposed to look dreadfully brave.
Not jolly of course—that would hardly be tactful,
  But . . . well, sort of loving and grave.

You are meant to believe that I simply don't care
  And am filled with a knowledge supernal,
Oh, well . . . about spiritual things, don't you know,
  Such as man being frightfully eternal.

This is my doodle-bug voice. Can you hear it?
  It's thrillingly vibrant, yet calm.
If we weren't in the office, which *isn't* the place,
  I'd read you a suitable psalm.

This is my doodle-bug place. Can you see me?
  It's really amazingly snug.
Lying under the desk with my doodle-bug face
  And my doodle-bug voice in the rug.

Virginia Graham

BOMB INCIDENT

Stretcher to stretcher still they came,
Young and old all looked the same—
Grimed and battered
Bleeding and shattered
And who they were it hardly mattered.
Where shall we put
The dogs and cat
The budgerigar
And the cricket bat?

Remnants of lives and forever lost days,
Families ended, minds that were dazed,
Clutched to the breast
Was all they had left
Of life that had gone and homes that were wrecked.
Where shall we put
The shopping bag
The picture of Grandma
The doll of rag?

Covered with dirt and with soot and with dust—
How to begin to clean them up,
To uncover the faces,
Identify people
When nothing is left of human features.
What shall we say
To the waiting friends?
How shall we know
Such anonymous ends?

And some are so still in the hospital beds
Who is dying and who is dead?
The dead must be moved
To make room for the living
But how tell the children tearfully clinging?
What can we say
As they call to a mother?
Or, dead on a stretcher,
A sister or brother.

Whom shall we blame for the folly of war?
Whom shall we tell these stories for?
Who will believe
The sadness of death,
The terror, the fear, and the emptiness—
What can they know
Of the vacant eyes
The sorrow too deep
In the heart that dies?

Barbara Catherine Edwards

POINT OF VIEW
(Heard in a butcher's shop, Bolton, Lancs.)

'It's slaughter—nothing more nor less—
The bombing in this war . . .
A dreadful thing . . . you'd never guess
The shocking sights we saw
In London, when the Blitz was on . . .
A leg hung from a tree;
A body with the top half gone
And nowt below the knee;
A hand with wedding ring and all;
Two feet in socks and boots;
A baby's head stuck to a shawl;
An arm torn by the roots;
While here and there was flesh in lumps
They shovelled into sacks.
It proper left us in the dumps . . .
Sent shivers down our backs.'

'It's slaughter, sir. I've seen a bit
Of what those swine can do.'
His chopper fell and fiercely split
A sheep's head clean in two.
'It's downright murder to attack
Defenceless folk who can't fight back!'
 . . . And swinging dumbly on a hook,
A dead pig gave him such a look.

R. P. Brett

THE LIFE THAT I HAVE

The life that I have
is all that I have,
   The life that I have is yours.

The love that I have
of the life that I have
   Is yours and yours and yours.

A sleep I shall have,
A rest I shall have
   Yet death will be but a pause.

For the peace of my years
In the long green grass
   Will be yours and yours and yours.

Leo Marks

*(Code poem used by Violette Szabo, the British Resistance
heroine who worked in France)*

PICTURE FROM THE BLITZ

After all these years
I can still close my eyes and see
her sitting there,
in her big armchair,
grotesque under an open sky,
framed by the jagged lines of her broken house.

Sitting there,
a plump homely person,
steel needles still in her work-rough hands;
grey with dust, stiff with shock,
but breathing,
no blood or distorted limbs;
breathing, but stiff with shock,
knitting unravelling on her apron'd knee.

They have taken the stretchers off my car
and I am running
under the pattering flack
over a mangled garden;
treading on something soft
and fighting the rising nausea—
only a far-flung cushion, bleeding feathers.

They lift her gently
out of her great armchair,
tenderly,
under the open sky,
a shock-frozen woman trailing khaki wool.

Lois Clark

AUTUMN BLITZ

Unshaken world! Another day of light
After the human chaos of the night;
Although a heart in mendless horror grieves,
What calmly yellow, gently falling leaves!

Frances Cornford

When the war is over
Hitler will be dead
He hopes to go to Heaven
With his halo on his head
But the Lord says NO
YOU'LL HAVE TO GO BELOW
THERE'S ONLY ROOM FOR CHURCHILL
SO CHEERY CHEERY OH!

WAR RHYMES
(Used for skipping or chanting by children)

Underneath the churchyard, six feet deep,
There lies Hitler fast asleep,
All the little mice come and tickle his feet,
'Neath the churchyard, six feet deep.

Who's that knocking at the window?
Who's that knocking at the door?
If it's Hitler, let him in
And we'll sit him on a pin,
And we won't see old Hitler any more.

Even Hitler had a mother,
Even Mussolini had a ma,
When they were babies they said Goo, goo, goo,
And sucked their thumbs, and got wet through.
Don't be hard upon the Blackshirts,
They may be rather Swastika,
              But
Even Hitler had a mother
              And
Even Mussolini had a ma.

SECOND AUTUMN

So here am I
  Upon the German earth, beneath the German sky,
  And birds flock southward, wheeling as they fly,
  And there are morning mists, and trees turn brown,
  And the winds blow, and blow the dead leaves down
  And lamps are earlier on, and curtains drawn,
  And nights have frosted dew-drops on the lawn,
  And bonfire smoke goes crawling up on high,
Just as on English earth, beneath an English sky.
But here am I.

    Patrick Savage

from *DUNKIRK*

All through the night, and in the next day's light
The endless columns came. Here was Defeat.
The men marched doggedly, and kept their arms,
But sleep weighed on their backs so that they reeled,
Staggering as they passed. Their force was spent.
Only, like old Horatius, each man saw
Far off his home, and seeing, plodded on.
At last they ceased. The sun shone down, and we
Were left to watch along a dusty road.

That night we blew our guns. We placed a shell
Fuse downwards in each muzzle. Then we put
Another in the breech, secured a wire
Fast to the firing lever, crouched, and pulled.
It sounded like a cry of agony,
The crash and clang of splitting, tempered steel.
Thus did our guns, our treasured colours, pass;
And we were left bewildered, weaponless,
And rose and marched, our faces to the sea.

We formed in line beside the water's edge.
The little waves made oddly home-like sounds,
Breaking in half-seen surf upon the strand.
The night was full of noise; the whistling thud
The shells made in the sand, and pattering stones;
The cries cut short, the shouts of units' names;
The crack of distant shots, and bren gun fire;
The sudden clattering crash of masonry.
Steadily, all the time, the marching tramp
Of feet passed by along the shell-torn road,
Under the growling thunder of the guns.
The major said 'The boats cannot get in,
'There is no depth of water. Follow me.'
And so we followed, wading in our ranks
Into the blackness of the sea. And there,
Lit by the burning oil across the swell,
We stood and waited for the unseen boats.

Oars in the darkness, rowlocks, shadowy shapes
Of boats that searched. We heard a seaman's hail.
Then we swam out, and struggled with our gear,
Clutching the looming gunwales. Strong hands pulled,
And we were in and heaving with the rest,
Until at last they turned. The dark oars dipped,
The laden craft crept slowly out to sea,
To where in silence lay the English ships.

B. G. Bonallack

WHEN THE PLANE DIVED

When the plane dived and the machine-gun spattered
The deck, in his numb clutch the tugging wheel
Bucked madly as he strove to keep the keel
Zig-zagging through the steep and choppy sea—
To keep zig-zagging, that was all that mattered . . .
To keep the ship zig-zagging endlessly,
Dodging that diving devil. Now again
The bullets spattered like a squall of rain
About him; and again with desperate grip
He tugged, to port the helm . . . to keep the ship
Zig-zagging . . . zig-zagging through eternity;
To keep the ship . . . A sudden scalding pain
Shot through his shoulder and the whole sky shattered
About him in red fire; and yet his grip
Tightened upon the wheel . . . To keep the ship . . .
Zig . . . zig . . . zig-zagging, that was all that mattered.

Wilfrid Gibson

from WEEKEND LEAVE

To waken slowly in this strange high-ceilinged room!
Cool wet winds lift the curtain's skirt;
Trees across the street nod to a sleep-eyed cloud,
Their foreheads glistening in the rain.

Today I shall have time to live,
To stop and watch people in streets, pigeons on roofs,
Children at play in parks, wheelbarrows and men digging,
Carthorses, the sheen of plough furrows like smooth hair, ponds,
Sparrows carrying crumbs, the art of well-laid hedges.

I shall have time to notice how the clouds
Build themselves up into turreted castles, fantastic beasts
Living upon their own vast mountain range;
I can listen to what the trees are saying,
Sit watching the language of your hands
Knitting, pouring tea, idly turning pages;
I can close my eyes and drink joy from your voice;
Walk hands in pockets, whistle in the woods,
Throw sticks for dogs or shout confusion amongst rooks.
Today I shall be a child,
Steal to catch a glimpse of fairies between trees.

An old tweed jacket hangs behind the door
Smelling of heather, tobacco, and burnt wood;
Coloured ties fall sprawled across the broad mirror,
And grey trousers loll in the deep arm-chair.

From down the hill where soiled shirt-sleeves
Take down the chalked-on black-out blinds,
Puff in and out their shops with shutters,
Where cold, red hands and smeared print aprons
Put vegetables in rows before their shops,
Down there in the world
(Like a bugle-call shaking me by the shoulder as I lie in bed)
Come the advancing chimes of city bells.
I can doze, and watch the clock tick round
Long past reveille, past the first parade,
And on and on, dragging
Shiny boots along the circle of an army day.

This afternoon we'll trace rabbits' paths like rail junctions,
Mark hares moving in arcs behind the woods and hills,
Raise a startled pheasant to go whirring
Over the stubble like a heavy bomber.
We'll sit on the broken stones of some old house
Standing in its briar-invaded garden.

We'll have tea at an old inn
Standing beckoning at the roadside—
A kindly old lady, in a shawl, smiling at a gate,
With wood fires and small square windows, bright curtains,
And flowers in pots on window-sills.

One more night in the careless freedom of that room.
Perhaps we will not wake up . . .
They have big warm farms in Warwickshire
And sloping lawns,
Gardens full of thick trees, lying stretched out
With their green legs dabbling in the Avon.
Perhaps next week we can go on the river,
Or lie all night
Amongst the clover in some Midland barn.

O God! Tomorrow I go back.

Richard Spender

AUTUMN LEAVES

The young soldier home on leave
  From his great gun
Sits by his wife's side
  In the autumn sun.

The tender words, the true,
  Will not be said,
They sit silent together
  And stare ahead.

That well-remembered song of love,
  So often sung,
Quivers but drowsily
  Upon the tongue.

The swift hours they share
  Are all too few,
Yet sleep drops on their eyes
  Like heavy dew.

Soon her lids close,
  Her head nods;
His mouth falls open a little
  Like a cod's.

The young soldier home on leave
  From his great gun
Sits by his wife's side
  In the autumn sun.

Virginia Graham

STEEL CATHEDRALS

It seems to me, I spend my life in stations.
Going, coming, standing, waiting.
Paddington, Darlington, Shrewsbury, York.
I know them all most bitterly.
Dawn stations, with a steel light, and waxen figures.
Dust, stone, and clanking sounds, hiss of weary steam.
Night stations, shaded light, fading pools of colour.
Shadows and the shuffling of a million feet.
Khaki, blue, and bulky kitbags, rifles gleaming dull.
Metal sound of army boots, and smoker's coughs.
Titter of harlots in their silver foxes.
Cases, casks, and coffins, clanging of the trolleys.
Tea urns tarnished, and the greasy white of cups.
Dry buns, Woodbines, Picture Post and Penguins;
and the blaze of magazines.
Grinding sound of trains, and rattle of the platform gates.
Running feet and sudden shouts, clink of glasses from the buffet.
Smell of drains, tar, fish and chips and sweaty scent, honk of taxis;
and the gleam of cigarettes.
Iron pillars, cupolas of glass, girders messed by pigeons;
the lazy singing of a drunk.
Sailors going to Chatham, soldiers going to Crewe.
Aching bulk of kit and packs, tin hats swinging.
The station clock with staggering hands and callous face,
says twenty-five-to-nine.
A cigarette, a cup of tea, a bun,
and my train goes at ten.

D. Van Den Bogaerde

117

from ON EMBARKATION

In all the ways of going who can tell
The real from the unjustified farewell?
Women have sobbed when children left for school
Or husbands took the boat train to pursue
Contracts more tenuous than the marriage vow.
But now each railway station makes and breaks
The certain hold and drifts us all apart.
Some women know exactly what's implied.
Ten Years, they say behind their smiling eyes,
Thinking of children, pensions, looks that fade,
The slow forgetfulness that strips the mind
Of its apparel and wears down the thread;
Or maybe when he laughs and bends to make
Her laugh with him she sees that he must die
Because his eyes declare it plain as day.
And it is here, if anywhere, that words
—Debased like money by the same diseases—
Cast off the habitual clichés of fatigue
—The women hoping it will soon blow over,
The fat men saying it depends on Russia—
And all are poets when they say Goodbye
And what they say will live and fructify.

Alun Lewis

Sheila carries daddy's gas-mask,
Peter carries daddy's gun.
Mother's chattering on and laughing
As if parting were just fun.

She's put apples in his pocket,
He's got photos in his book,
When he isn't busy fighting,
He'll have time to have a look.

118

BEWARE

HE WANTS TO KNOW YOUR UNIT'S NAME,
WHERE YOU'RE GOING, WHENCE YOU CAME,
EVEN ALONE OR IN A CROWD
NEVER MENTION THESE OUT LOUD.

HOW TO KILL

Under the parabola of a ball,
a child turning into a man,
I looked into the air too long.
The ball fell in my hand, it sang
in the closed fist: *Open, open*
Behold a gift designed to kill.

Now in my dial of glass appears
the soldier who is going to die.
He smiles, and moves about in ways
his mother knows, habits of his.
The wires touch his face; I cry
NOW. Death, like a familiar, hears

and look, has made a man of dust
of a man of flesh. This sorcery
I do. Being damned, I am amused
to see the centre of love diffused
and the waves of love travel into vacancy.
How easy it is to make a ghost.

The weightless mosquito touches
her tiny shadow on the stone,
and with how like, how infinite
a likeness, man and shadow meet.
They fuse. A shadow is a man
when the mosquito death approaches.

Keith Douglas

from BURMA CASUALTY
(To Captain G. T. Morris, Indian Army)

'Your leg must go. Okay?' the surgeon said
'Take it' he said. 'I hate the bloody thing.'
Yet he was terrified—not of the knives
Nor loosing that green leg (he'd often wished
He'd had a gun to shoot the damned thing off)
But of the darkness that he knew would come
And bid him enter its deep gates alone.

The nurse would help him and the orderlies.
But did they know? And could a rubber tube
Suck all that darkness out of lungs and heart?
'Open and close your fist—slowly,' the doctor said.
He did so, lying still upon his back.
The whitewashed walls, the windows bright with sky
Gathered a brilliant light above his head.
Here was the light, the promise hard and pure,
His wife's sweet body and her wilful eyes.
Her timeless love stooped down to raise him up.
He felt the white walls part—the needle pricked,
'Ten seconds and you'll fade,' the doctor said.
He lay and looked into the snowwhite skies
For all ten seconds means at such a time.
Then through the warped interstices of life
The darkness swept like water through a boat
In gouts and waves of softness, claiming him . . .

He went alone: knew nothing: and returned
Retching and blind with pain, and yet Alive.

Alun Lewis

L.R.D.G.

He threw his cigarette in silence, then he said:

You can't predict in war;
It's a matter of luck, nothing less, nothing more.
Now here's an instance. Darnley copped it in the head
His third day up the blue although he'd seen the lot
In Dunkerque, Greece and Crete—
The sort that went in tidy and came out neat;
He copped it when the going wasn't even hot.
And there was little Pansy Flowers,
Machine-gunned through the guts; he bled
(And not a murmur from him) for hours
Before he jagged it in.

                        And you remember Bowers?
Bowers got fragmentation in the lungs and thigh;
We couldn't do a thing: the moon was high
And a hell of a bright
On that particular night.
Poor sod, he won't kip in a civvy bed.

It's queer . . . I've even laughed
When blokes have chucked it in and gone daft.
I remember one that scarpered bollock-nude
One midnight, out across the dunes, calling for Mum;
You'd have thought him blewed.
He wasn't seen again—not this side of Kingdom Come.

One job that I really funked
Was when Fat Riley bunked
From a Jerry leaguer on a getaway.
We found him blind, with both hands gone.
When we got him back inside the lines
He'd only say,
Over and over, 'the mines, the mines, the mines'.
It's the lucky ones get dead:
He's still alive. I wonder if his wife understands
How you can't even shoot yourself without your hands.

J. G. Meddemmen

122

STILL NO LETTER . . .

There's still no letter . . .
                    In my troubled mind
I seek a reason, and quickly reasons find,
Indeed they tumble in, to be discarded
Each as it comes . . . It could be that
You're very busy; missed the evening post;
Or else it's held up in the mail. A host
Of explanations . . . Yet that gnawing fear
O'errides them, still keeps dunning at me that
You just don't want to write. And vainly I
Attempt to thrust aside the thought; deny
It with your last note, and the one before.
But no. I must resign myself to wait
Until tomorrow, or the next day and
A day. Surely then I see your hand—
Writing and envelope. And life is sweet, until
A week or so, when . . .
                    Still no letter.

John Wedge

TOAST

All the way back from the air field
Along the jolting road,
Past the paddy fields
And the mud-covered water-buffalo,
I have been pretending to myself
That I am not thinking about letters.
At the door of Regulating I pause,
It is a creed with me never to look for a letter,
If there is one for me it will find me.
Today, feeling bad-tempered, I defy my creed
But there is no letter.
I walk up to the mess.
Irrationally I can feel hot tears in my eyes.
I concentrate on the thought of toast for tea,
Hot toast and lots of butter,
Even jam.
It is something to look forward to for almost ten minutes.
No one answers when I speak,
They are deep in their letters.
I pour milk into my tea and wait for the toast.
They laugh over their letters, and read excerpts,
From a sister in Australia,
From a friend in hospital,
From a friend in France,
I think hard about the toast.
There is no jam but meat paste
And a soft-looking paw-paw which I don't like.
The toast is as good as I know it will be
I crunch it slowly
And the butter runs on to my fingers
And I try not to listen to Wren shop,
To the details of the friend's illness,
To the delinquencies of the dhobi.
I am a little afraid, for when the toast is finished
There will be nothing to look forward to,
And so it was yesterday
And so it will be tomorrow.

Olivia FitzRoy

THE SOLDIERS AT LAURO

Young are the dead
Like babies they lie
The wombs they blest once
Not healed dry
And yet—too soon
Into each space
A cold earth falls
On colder face.
Quite still they lie
These fresh reeds
Clutched in earth
Like winter seeds
But these will not bloom
When called by spring
To burst with leaf
And blossoming.
They will sleep on
In silent dust
As crosses rot
And memories rust.

Spike Milligan

DEAD GERMAN YOUTH

He lay there, mutilated and forlorn,
Save that his face was woundless, and his hair
Drooped forward and caressed his boyish brow.
He looked so tired, as if his life had been
Too full of pain and anguish to endure,
And like a weary child who tires of play
He lay there, waiting for decay.
I feel no anger towards you, German boy,
Whom war has driven down the path of pain.
Would God we could have met in peace
And laughed and talked with tankards full of beer,
For I would rather hear your youthful mirth
At stories which I often loved to tell
Than stand here looking down at you
So terrible, so quiet and so still.

C. P. S. Denholm-Young

KILLED IN ACTION

For N. J. De B.-L.
Crete, May, 1941

His chair at the table, empty,
His home clothes hanging in rows forlorn,
His cricket bat and cap, his riding cane,
The new flannel suit he had not worn.
His dogs, restless, with tortured ears
Listening for his swift, light tread upon the path.
And there—his violin! Oh his violin! Hush! hold your tears.

Juliette de Bairacli-Levy

LADY IN BLACK

Lady in black,
I knew your son.
Death was our enemy
Death and his gun.

Death had a trench
And he blazed away.
We took that trench
By the end of the day.

Lady in black
Your son was shot.
He was my mate
And he got it hot.

Death's a bastard
Keeps hitting back.
But a war's a war
Lady in black

Birth hurt bad
But you didn't mind.
Well maybe Death
Can be just as kind.

So take it quiet
The same as your son.
Death's only a vicar
Armed with a gun.

And one day Death
Will give it back
And then you can speak to him tidy
Lady in black.

Alun Lewis

LAMENT

We knelt on the rocks by the dark green pools
The sailor boy and I,
And we dabbled our hands in the weed-veined water
Under a primrose sky.
And we laughed together to hide the sorrow
Of words we left unsaid;
Then he went back to his dirty minesweeper
And I to a lonely bed.
O the anguish of tears unshed.

And never again on this earth shall we meet,
The sailor boy and I,
And never again shall I see his face
Framed in a primrose sky,
For the sea has taken his laughter and loving
And buried him dark and deep
And another lad sleeps on the dirty minesweeper
A sleep that I cannot sleep.
O that I could forget and weep.

Frances Mayo

WAR

When the bloom is off the garden,
and I'm fighting in the sky,
when the lawns and flower beds harden,
and when weak birds starve and die,
and death-roll will grow longer,
eyes will be moist and red;
and the more I kill, the longer
shall I miss friends who are dead.

Nigel Weir

128

FAMILY GROUP
(*Familiale*)

The mother has her knitting
The son has his fighting
She finds this quite natural the mother does
And the father has what has the father got?
He has his business
His wife has her knitting
His son his fighting
And he his business
He thinks this quite natural the father does
And the son and the son
What does the son make of this?
He makes precisely nothing does the son
The son's mother has her knitting his father his business and he his
    fighting
And when he has finished his fighting
He will go to business with his father
The fighting goes on the mother goes on knitting
The father goes on going to business
The son is killed he doesn't go on
The father and the mother go to the funeral
They find this quite natural the father and mother do
Life goes on life with knitting fighting business
Business fighting knitting fighting
Business business business
Life and the business of funerals

Jacques Prévert
Trans. A. S. J. Tessimond

WHEN THEY SOUND THE LAST ALL-CLEAR,
How happy my darling we'll be,
When they turn up the lights
And the dark lonely nights,
Are only a memory,
Never more we'll be apart,
Always together sweetheart,
For the peace bells will ring
And the whole world will sing
WHEN THEY SOUND THE LAST ALL-CLEAR.

THE YEAR AFTER

Boys were playing at marbles
in the spring mud behind a cart.
Girls skipping rope in sunshine.
Kari did not take part.

Why don't you join us, Kari?
And then the girl quickly said:
—I don't want to play with you any more.
She quietly turned her head.

A German came down the road.
Children's faces set.
Kari defiant, straight as a rod!
Her eyes shone clear and wet.

The German on the road
Softly stroked her blonde hair.
The soldier's steel helmet glittered.
Guttural, strange his words were;

—Ach Himmel, solch ein Mädchen
hatt 'ich im deutschen land.—
Quietly turned away from her
his eye to the roadside went.

He straightened up, weary and cold.
No smile. No answer. He knew.
Judged by two clear bright eyes:
—I once had a father too.

Tormod Skagestad
Trans. Martin Allwood

PEBBLE

I know a man who's got a pebble.

He found it and he sucked it
during the war.
He found it and he sucked it
when they ran out of water.
He found it and he sucked it
when they were dying for a drink.
And he sucked it and he sucked it
for days and days and days.

I know a man who's got a pebble
and he keeps it in his drawer.

It's small and brown—nothing much to look at
but I think of the things he thinks
when he sees it:
how he found it
how he sucked it
how he nearly died for water to drink.

A small brown pebble
tucked under his tongue
and he keeps it in his drawer
to look at now and then.

Michael Rosen

THE RAIN

When my older brother
came back from war
he had on his forehead a little silver star
and under the star
an abyss

a splinter of shrapnel
hit him at Verdun
or perhaps at Grünwald
(he'd forgotten the details)

he used to talk much
in many languages
but he liked most of all
the language of history

until losing breath
he commanded his dead pals to run
Roland Kowalski Hannibal

he shouted
that this was the last crusade
that Carthage soon would fall
and then sobbing confessed
that Napoleon did not like him

we looked at him
getting paler and paler
abandoned by his senses
he turned slowly into a monument

into musical shells of ears
entered a stone forest
and the skin of his face
was secured
with the blind dry
buttons of eyes
nothing was left him
but touch

what stories
he told with his hands
in the right he had romances
in the left soldier's memories

they took my brother
and carried him out of town
he returns every fall
slim and very quiet
(he does not want to come in)
he knocks at the window for me

we walk together in the streets
and he recites to me
improbable tales
touching my face
with blind fingers of rain

Zbigniew Herbert
Trans. Czeslaw Milosz

POST-WAR

In 1943
my father
dropped bombs on the continent

I remember
my mother
talking about bananas
in 1944

when it rained,
creeping alone to the windowsill,
I stared up the hill,
watching, watching,
watching without a blink
for the Mighty Bananas
to stride through the blitz

they came in paper bags
in neighbours' hands
when they came
and took their time
over the coming

and still I don't know
where my father
flying home
took a wrong turning

Libby Houston

IN EVERY STREET

In every street I thought of my father and mother
I did not walk there alone when I was a child
without me they must have walked closer to each other
I am nearly their age now and know that they were not old

Where today the heart of the town pumps tramcars and buses
every symbol stresses the travellers' freedom of choice
in this bantam metropolis who is concerned what uses
have been found for the buses which transported the Jews

In my native town I cannot walk like a stranger
all that remains to me of my parents is the truth
their death foreshortens as my shadow grows longer
my life has more space for them now than it had in my youth

Karen Gershon

WILL IT BE SO AGAIN?

Will it be so again
That the brave, the gifted are lost from view,
And empty, scheming men
Are left in peace their lunatic age to renew?
Will it be so again?

Must it be always so
That the best are chosen to fall and sleep
Like seeds, and we too slow
In claiming the earth they quicken, and the old usurpers reap
What they could not sow?

Will it be so again—
The jungle code and the hypocrite gesture?
A poppy wreath for the slain
And a cut-throat world for the living? that stale imposture
Played on us once again?

Will it be as before—
Peace, with no heart or mind to ensue it,
Guttering down to war
Like a libertine to his grave? We should not be surprised: we knew
  it
Happen before

Shall it be so again?
Call not upon the glorious dead
To be your witnesses then.
The living alone can nail to their promise the ones who said
It shall not be so again.

    C. Day Lewis

INDEX OF FIRST LINES

BIOGRAPHICAL NOTES
First World War

HERBERT ASQUITH Born 1881, son of the First Earl of Oxford and Asquith, who was Prime Mininster in 1914. Educated at Winchester and Balliol College, Oxford and at Lincoln's Inn, he was called to the Bar in 1907. He served in France and Flanders from 1915–18, as a captain in the Royal Field Artillery. The most recent collection of his poetry was published by Sidgwick and Jackson in 1940. He died in 1947. (SEE p26)

LAURENCE BINYON Born in 1869 in Lancaster. Educated at St Paul's School and Trinity College, Oxford. Joined the staff of the British Museum in 1893 and from 1913–33 was keeper of Oriental Prints and Drawings. As well as writing his own poetry he compiled anthologies and wrote books on art. He died in 1943. *Collected Poems* published by Macmillan. (SEE p58)

VERA BRITTAIN Born in Staffordshire in 1893. Her education at Somerville College, Oxford was interrupted when she enlisted as a VAD nurse, serving in London, Malta and France. She returned to Oxford after the war in which her fiancé, her brother, and many friends died. She became a dedicated pacifist, joining the Peace Pledge Union in 1937. She married the political philosopher, G. E. Catlin and had two children, one of whom is Shirley Williams, the politician. Vera Brittain travelled widely, writing and lecturing, and published twenty nine books, among them *Testament of Youth*, and *Chronicle of Youth* about the First World War (dramatized for television) and *England's Hour* about the Second World War. She died in 1970. (SEE pp57, 59)

RUPERT BROOKE Born in 1887 and educated at Rugby where his father was a housemaster and at King's College, Cambridge. His thesis on the Jacobean dramatist John Webster gained him a University Fellowship and he had already published some poetry before he enlisted in August 1914. Winston Churchill offered him a commission in the Royal Naval Division, and his experiences at Antwerp in October 1914 led to his writing the five war sonnets. Early in 1915 on the way to Gallipoli he contracted pneumonia and died of acute blood poisoning on 23rd April, St George's Day. His grave is on the Island of Skyros. Brooke was once called 'the handsomest young man in England' and was much admired. His sonnet 'The Soldier' became one of the war's most popular poems and was read by the Dean of St Paul's before the Sunday sermon, three weeks before Brooke's death. *Collected Poems* published by Sidgwick and Jackson. (SEE pp14, 16)

T. P. CAMERON WILSON A captain in the Sherwood Foresters who had been a schoolmaster before the war. He was killed in France in 1918. His poetry was originally published by the Poetry Bookshop in London but is now, except for some anthologized pieces, out of print. (SEE p48)

JOHN DRINKWATER Born London, 1882 and educated at Oxford High School and Birmingham University. He worked in insurance for twelve years, but was always fascinated by the theatre. During the war he acted and stage-managed at the Birmingham Repertory Theatre. As well as poetry for both adults and children, he wrote several successful plays. He died in 1937. (SEE p21)

ELEANOR FARJEON Born in London, 1881, daughter of novelist B. L. Farjeon and a grand-daughter of Joseph Jefferson, the American actor. With no formal education, she and her three brothers had an imaginative upbringing which included books, theatre, music and art. She knew many leading writers well, including D. H. Lawrence, and fell in love with Edward Thomas, contenting herself with encouraging his poetry and becoming a friend to his wife and children. She became one of the most popular children's writers publishing more than eighty books of stories, poetry, plays and autobiography, including *Edward Thomas: The Last Four Years* (1958). She won several major literary awards. Became a Catholic in 1951, and died in 1965. (SEE p55)

F. S. FLINT Frank Stewart Flint was born in 1885. He had little formal education but became a leading member of a group of poets known as the Imagists, and was an early writer of free verse. He frequented the Poetry Bookshop in London, a centre for poets and poetry readings. From 1920 onwards he devoted himself to working for the Civil Service, wrote no more poetry, but concentrated on the translation and criticism of French poetry, for which he was highly regarded. He died in 1960. (SEE pp20, 36)

WILFRID WILSON GIBSON Born in Northumberland in 1878. Came to London where his poetry soon gained popularity and he became one of the leading Georgian poets. Poor eyesight prevented his enlisting, but he served with the RASC in this country. Gibson was one of the only poets to write during both world wars and died in 1962, aged eighty-four. (SEE pp18, 29, 44, 45, 62, 86, 98, 113)

ROBERT GRAVES Born in London in 1895. Son of an Irish poet and editor, A. P. Graves. Educated at Charterhouse and St John's College, Oxford. Served in France with the Royal Welsh Fusiliers and was a friend of Sassoon and Owen. Actually reported as 'died of wounds' on his twenty-first birthday, Graves in fact survived the war to become one of the best-known and most prolific poets of his generation, although he rather disregarded his war poetry. His account of the war, *Goodbye To All That* is highly regarded and he wrote several novels on historical, religious and classical themes including *I, Claudius* (also a popular TV series) and *King Jesus*. From 1929 he lived in Majorca, travelling frequently to America to lecture and to England where he was made Oxford Professor of Poetry in 1961. Graves won several major awards and died in 1985, aged 90. (SEE pp23, 28)

IVOR GURNEY Born 1890 in Gloucester. Awarded a scholarship for composition to the Royal College of Music in 1911. Served on the Western Front as a private from 1915–17 and was wounded and gassed. After the war he was frequently in a disturbed mental state, and from 1922 onwards spent his life under care, but he continued to compose fine music, particularly settings of Edward Thomas's and A. E. Housman's poetry, and went on writing poetry. Interest in him has grown considerably. He died in the City of London Mental Hospital in 1937. *Collected Poems* published by Oxford University Press. (SEE p30)

MAY HERSCHEL CLARKE (SEE p44)

TERESA HOOLEY Born in 1888. *Selected Poems* published by Jonathan Cape. Her poetry also appeared in the *Sunday Times* and the *Observer*. She died in April 1973. (SEE pp35, 61)

A. E. HOUSMAN Born Bromsgrove, Worcestershire in 1859 and educated at Bromsgrove School and St John's College, Oxford. Worked as a clerk in the Patent Office, London. In 1892 was appointed Professor of Latin at London University and gained a reputation as a classicist. In 1896 he published *A Shropshire Lad* at his own expense, and these poems grew immensely popular during the war years. He continued to write poetry after the war. He died in 1936. His *Collected Poems* is published by Jonathan Cape. (SEE p54)

RUDYARD KIPLING Born 1865 in Bombay. Educated at Hope House, Southsea and United Services College, Westward Ho!. Returned to India at the age of seventeen to work as a journalist. He began writing verse and stories, which soon became popular. He married an American, Caroline Starr Balestier and lived for a while in the States, and returned to England in 1896. In 1907 he was awarded the Nobel Prize for literature. He died in 1936 and is buried in Poets' Corner in Westminster Abbey. His best-known works are *Just So Stories*, *The Jungle Book*, *Kim* and *Puck of Pook's Hill*, and his various collections of short stories. (SEE p31)

ROSE MACAULAY Born 1889 in Cambridge and went to school and college in Oxford. Her early enthusiasm about the war soon faded. She became a well-respected novelist, essayist and poet, winning several literary prizes and became a Dame of the British Empire. She was a member of the Bloomsbury Group and a friend of Rupert Brooke in her youth. Died 1958 (SEE pp22, 34)

JOHN McCRAE Born at Guelph, Ontario, in 1892. Educated at the University of Toronto. Fellow in Pathology at McGill University and Montreal General Hospital. Served in the Canadian Contingent in the South African War and went to Europe as a gunner, later as a medical officer in 1914. His well-loved poem 'In Flanders Field' first appeared in *Punch* in 1915. It was only after his death, of pneumonia, in 1918 that his poems were collected and published (Hodder & Stoughton, 1919). (SEE p50)

NINA MACDONALD (SEE p32)

BEATRICE MAYOR (SEE p50)

A. A. MILNE Born 1882 and educated at Westminster and Trinity College, Cambridge. He was Assistant Editor of *Punch* from 1906–14, then fought with the Royal Warwickshire Regiment at the Battle of the Somme. His war verse was originally published in *Punch*, and he wrote many plays, sketches, novels and essays. His most popular work has remained *When We Were Very Young*

(1924), *Winnie The Pooh* (1926), *Now We Are Six* (1927), *The House at Pooh Corner* (1928)*, and his dramatization of Kenneth Grahame's *The Wind in the Willows*, called *Toad of Toad Hall*, in 1929. A. A. Milne became a pacifist and died in 1956. (SEE pp58, 68)

ERNO MULLER (SEE p25)

WILFRED OWEN Born at Oswestry in 1893. Educated at Birkenhead Institute and the University of London. Interested in literature from boyhood, and Keats and French poetry were early influences. He worked as a tutor in Bordeaux from 1913–15, then enlisted in the Artists Rifles and was commissioned in the Manchester Regiment, June 1916. After serving in the trenches from January to June 1917 he was posted home on sick leave. At Craiglockhart hospital, near Edinburgh, he met Sassoon and was influenced and encouraged by the older poet. In September 1918 he returned to active service in France and was awarded the Military Cross in the October. He was killed in action on 4th November 1918, exactly one week before the Armistice. Owen has become the best-known poet of the First World War. His *Collected Poems* opens with a much quoted Preface: 'This book is not about heroes. English poetry is not yet fit to speak of them . . . My subject is War, and the Pity of War. The Poetry is in the pity.' *Collected Poems* published by Chatto and Windus. (SEE pp13, 43, 54, 56)

MARGARET POSTGATE COLE Born in Cambridge in 1893 and educated at Roedean and Girton College, Cambridge. Taught classics at St Paul's school before working for the Fabian Society and marrying G. D. H. Cole, the labour historian and economist. Together they wrote many political books and detective novels. Chairman of the Further Education Committee of London County Council in 1950, and a Dame of the British Empire. Died in 1980. (SEE pp21, 56)

CONSTANCE POWELL (SEE p60)

HERBERT READ Born at Kirbymoorside, Yorkshire in 1893 and educated at Crossley School, Halifax and Leeds University. Was with the Green Howards 1915–18, made a captain in 1917. From 1922–31 he was Keeper of the Victoria and Albert Museum, London before settling to a career of writing. As well as his poetry he wrote on art and literature and was knighted in 1953. He died in 1968. *Collected Poems* published by Faber. (SEE pp37, 72)

EDGELL RICKWORD Born in 1898 and joined the Artists Rifles when eighteen years old in 1916. He lost an eye while fighting on the Western Front, and was invalided out. He became a noted literary critic, later turning more to political writing. He died in 1982. *Collected Poems* published by the Bodley Head. (SEE p24)

ISAAC ROSENBERG Born Bristol, 1890, of Jewish parentage, his parents being emigrés from Russia. The family moved to London's East End where Isaac went to school, learned painting and began to write poetry. At fourteen he became apprenticed to an engraver, but in 1911 another Jewish family paid for him to attend the Slade School of Art. Early published writing went unnoticed and in 1915, despite the family's pacifist views, he joined the army. He went to the trenches as a private in 1916 and was killed in action in 1918. It has taken time for his painting and poetry to receive the notice it deserves. (SEE p46)

SIEGFRIED SASSOON Born 1886 and educated at Marlborough and Clare College, Cambridge. He served with the Royal Welsh Fusiliers where his courage was notable; he was nicknamed 'Mad Jack' and won the Military Cross (which he later threw away). He wrote his war poetry at the front and was one of the first poets to show contempt for the war leaders, and to describe the horror of the trenches. Suffering from shell shock he was taken to hospital at Craiglockhart, where he met Wilfred Owen. Sassoon was one of the few poets to survive the war. He became Literary Editor of the *Daily Herald* in 1919, continuing to write poetry, and his autobiographies both won prizes—*Memoirs of a Fox-Hunting Man* won the Hawthornden Prize and *Memoirs of an Infantry Officer* the James Tait Black Memorial Prize. In later life he became a Catholic. He was awarded the CBE in 1951. His *Diaries*, *War Poems* and *Collected Poems*, all edited by Rupert Hart-Davis, are published by Faber. He died in 1967. (SEE pp24, 42, 47, 52, 59, 62)

VERNON SCANNELL Born in Spilsby, Lincolnshire in 1922 and educated at Queens Park School, Aylesbury, Buckinghamshire and the University of Leeds, 1946–7. Although he in fact only served in the Second World War, the poem included here is about the First World War. He served in the Gordon Highlanders in the

Middle East and Normandy where he was wounded. He lived in many parts of England before settling in Yorkshire in 1980. He has five children and has worked as a teacher of English as well as once being a boxer. Since 1962 he has been a freelance writer and broadcaster, and has won several literary awards. His interest in poetry came after his schooldays and his varied experiences have taught him that young people are able to respond to quite painful, disturbing themes. He has written novels, plays and books on poetry, and his *Collected Poems* is published by Robson Books. (SEE p13)

ALAN SEEGER Born 1888 in New York. Lived in Mexico as a child then studied at Harvard. After visiting Paris in 1912–13 he came to London to research at the British Museum Library and joined the French Foreign Legion at the outbreak of the war. He was killed at the Somme on 4th July 1916, Independence Day in the USA. His death, and in particular the poem 'I Have a Rendezvous With Death', brought him fame and popularity. (SEE p19)

CHARLES HAMILTON SORLEY Born in 1895. Educated at Marlborough. He spent a year in Germany, then returned to England to enlist in the army. He was made an officer at the start of the war and died after six months in the trenches in France in 1915. For a long time his poetry remained neglected, but is now reaching a wider public. A collection of his poetry is published by Cecil Woolf. (SEE p47)

EDWARD THOMAS Born in London on 3rd March 1878 of Welsh parentage. He always loved the countryside and at St Paul's School wrote on the fly-leaf of his algebra book: 'I love birds more than books.' Married Helen Noble while still an undergraduate at Lincoln College, Oxford, and with three children to provide for was often forced into arduous journalistic work. Until 1914 he wrote mainly prose but, encouraged by the American poet Robert Frost, and his friend Eleanor Farjeon, he began to write poetry at the start of the war. In 1915 he enlisted in the Artists Rifles and went on active service early in 1917. Although he did not write directly of warfare and trench horrors, war inspires and touches many of his poems. Thomas was killed by the blast from a passing shell at Arras on 9th April 1917. *Collected Poems* published by Oxford University Press and Faber. (SEE pp17, 55)

HUMBERT WOLFE Born in Milan in 1885 and educated at Bradford Grammar School and Wadham College, Oxford. Was Principal Assistant Secretary at the Ministry of Labour and was awarded the CBE in 1925. A prolific writer of light and serious verse, as well as essays, critical studies and plays. Well-known titles include *Kensington Gardens* (1924), *This Blind Rose* (1928) and *Snow* (1931). He died in 1940 (SEE p49)

W. B. YEATS Born in Dublin 1865 and educated at Godolphin School, Hammersmith, and in Dublin. Studied Art and also helped to establish the Irish National Theatre in 1899. He became recognized as the leader of the Irish Literary movement and was awarded the Nobel Prize for Literature in 1923. In his middle years he became fascinated by the occult. He continued writing until his last years and died in 1939. His *Collected Poems* is published by Macmillan. (SEE p17)

VALENTINE ACKLAND Born 1906 and educated at Queens College, London and in Paris. During the war she served as a civil defence clerk in Dorset. Was converted to Catholicism in 1946, and died in 1969. (SEE p75)

BASIL G. BONALLACK Born 1907. Educated Mill Hill and Clare College, Cambridge. Served with the Honourable Artillery Company 92nd Field Regiment Royal Artillery. Took part in major battles in Europe. His poem 'Dunkirk' was started in France in 1940 and completed on the Anzio beach-head three years later. (SEE p111)

DAVID BOURNE Born 1921, Meopham, Kent and educated at Cranbrook. He was a pilot officer in the RAF and left behind about 140 poems. About half were published by the Bodley Head in 1944; others appeared in a collection of poems by public school boys who died in the war, called *For Your Tomorrow* (OUP 1950). That title was translated from a verse on the memorial to the 2nd Division at Kohima.

> When you go home tell them of us and say
> For your tomorrow we gave our today.

David Bourne was shot down and killed, aged twenty, on 5th September 1941. (SEE p72)

R. P. BRETT (SEE p105)

CHARLES CAUSLEY Born Launceston, Cornwall in 1917 and educated at Launceston Grammar School, Launceston College and Peterborough College. The Cornish landscape and the sea made a deep early impression on him. He served in the Royal Navy from 1940–46, then taught in Cornwall until 1976. He retired from teaching to write full-time and give poetry readings and broadcasts here and abroad. He has been Honorary Visiting Fellow in Poetry at Exeter University, and a member of the Arts Council Literature Panel, and has won several awards for his writing. As well as many volumes of poetry for adults and children he has written plays and edited some anthologies. *Collected Poems*, and more recently *Secret Destinations*, are published by Macmillan. (SEE p87)

LOIS CLARK Studied dance and drama and then worked on stage and television. Worked as an ambulance driver during the war. Married in 1941. Has written poetry since a teenager and now lives in St Albans. She is a member of Vers Poets. (SEE p107)

HERBERT CORBY Born London 1911. In the 1930s was published in the magazine *Comment*, edited by Victor Neuberg. He thought himself that his best poetry was written when he served in an RAF Bomber squadron. After the war he worked with the Foreign Service. *Hampdens Going Over* was published by Editions Poetry London in 1945. (SEE p71)

FRANCES CORNFORD Born 1886 in Cambridge, daughter of Sir Francis Darwin and grand-daughter of Charles Darwin. Educated at home, married Francis Cornford, Fellow of Trinity College, Cambridge. She was a close friend of Rupert Brooke. The eldest of her five children was John Cornford, the poet who died in the Spanish Civil War. As well as her own poetry she translated poems from Russian. A poet who has not had the recognition she merits. She died in 1960. Her most recent *Collected Poems* was published by the Cresset Press in 1955. (SEE p108)

C. DAY LEWIS Born Ireland 1904. Educated at Sherborne, and Wadham College, Oxford, where he associated with a group of left-wing poets led by W. H. Auden. A schoolmaster for a time, he was politically active during the '30s, but turned from political to pastoral and lyrical poetry in later years. As well as his poetry he had a successful career writing detective fiction under the pseudonym, Nicholas Blake. He was firmly established as a leading literary figure in the '40s and frequently lectured, broadcast and gave poetry readings, becoming Professor of Poetry at Oxford from 1951–56. In 1968 he was appointed Poet Laureate. He died in 1972. *Collected Poems* published by Jonathan Cape and the Hogarth Press. (SEE p135)

JULIETTE DE BAIRACLI-LEVY Born in Manchester. Her father was Turkish and her mother was Egyptian. Educated at Withington Girls' High School, Manchester, and Lowther College, Wales. She then went on to study biology and veterinary medicine at Manchester and Liverpool Universities but did not complete her studies. She served in the Women's Land Army during the war. Her brother and childhood sweetheart, along with many French relatives, died in the holocaust. She now lives in Kythera, Greece. (SEE p126)

C. P. S. DENHOLM-YOUNG Colonel. Commanded the Signal Regiment of the 51st Highland Division. After the war returned to accountancy and is now a genealogist. (SEE p126)

KEITH DOUGLAS Born 1920 in Tunbridge Wells. Educated Christ's Hospital and Merton College, Oxford. His verse appeared in magazines in the '30s but the only volume published in his lifetime was *Selected Poems* (1943), while he was serving with the Sherwood Rangers Yeomanry. He fought in a crusader tank from Alamein to Tunisia and wrote a prose account of tank-warfare in the desert, *Alamein to Zem-Zem*. Promoted to captain and killed by enemy artillery fire on his third day in Normandy, June 1944. Desmond Graham wrote his biography and edited the *Collected Poems* (both published by OUP). (SEE pp84, 120)

BARBARA CATHERINE EDWARDS Her collection *Poems from Hospital* was published by Outposts Publications in 1962. (SEE p103)

OLIVIA FITZROY Born in 1921 in Christchurch, Hampshire. Her father was Captain the Hon. R. O. FitzRoy, later to be Viscount Daventry. When the war began she worked in the library of a London store, and then joined the Women's Royal Naval Service. She served as a flight direction officer first in Yeovilton and then in Ceylon. Her boyfriend, who was a pilot, was killed towards the end of the war. She married Sir Geoffrey Bates in 1957 and had two daughters. She wrote prolifically from childhood and published nine books in all, including the official history of the 8th King's Royal Irish Hussars, 1927–58. Died in 1969. (SEE pp83, 124)

KAREN GERSHON Born 1923 in Bielefeld, Germany. Came to England as a refugee in 1938. Both her parents died in concentration camps. She began writing poetry in English in 1950. In 1969 she went to Jerusalem where she lived with her four children until 1973. She was awarded the *Jewish Chronicle* Book Prize in 1967 and the Pioneer Women Poetry Award in 1968. She has five collections of poetry published. She now lives in St Austell, Cornwall. (SEE p134)

WILFRID WILSON GIBSON (SEE FIRST WORLD WAR)

VIRGINIA GRAHAM Born 1910. Daughter of the well-known

humorous writer Harry Graham. Educated at Notting Hill High School and then privately. Worked during the war with the Women's Voluntary Service. Married Anthony Thesiger. A contributor to *Punch* and other periodicals. Film critic for the *Spectator* from 1946–56. *Consider the Years*, her collection of war poetry, is published by Jonathan Cape. (SEE pp88, 102, 116)

ADRIAN HENRI Born Birkenhead, 1932, and studied fine art at the University of Durham. Settled in Liverpool in 1957 and in the '60s was associated with Roger McGough and Brian Patten as one of the Liverpool Poets. Since 1970 has been a freelance poet, painter, singer, songwriter and lecturer, touring Europe and the USA. His paintings have been widely exhibited, and he has published poetry for children and adults. *Collected Poems* published by Allison and Busby. (SEE p66)

ZBIGNIEW HERBERT Born in 1924 in Poland. He was over thirty when his first book of poetry was published. He was a member of the underground movement in Poland during the war. He has a diploma in law and also studied philosophy and history of art. He now lives in Warsaw. *Selected Poems* published by Carcanet. (SEE p133)

STANLEY HOLLOWAY Born 1890 and was originally a seaside concert artist. First appeared on the London stage in 1919, and performed in scores of plays, musical comedies, pantomimes, films and solo performances on both sides of the Atlantic. He performed his famous monologues, including several about 'young Albert' between 1929–41. He continued to make records and appear on TV until his death in 1982. (SEE p78)

LIBBY HOUSTON Born 1941 in north London. Educated at Oxford University. She had been writing poetry for twenty years and is a regular contributor to the BBC Schools Radio series *Pictures in Your Mind*. She has been a tutor for the Arvon Foundation since 1976 and has recently set up a poetry workshop in Bristol, where she now lives. Her collections *A Stained Glass Raree Show*, *Plain Clothes* and *At the Mercy* are published by Allison and Busby. (SEE p133)

RANDALL JARRELL American poet and critic. Born Nashville, Tennessee, 1914. For many years taught in various colleges, and wrote a satirical novel on campus life, *Pictures from an Institution*. His books for children *The Animal Family* and *The Bat Poet* have an unusual haunting quality. He published several volumes of poetry. *Collected Poems* published by Faber. (SEE p67)

ELIZABETH JENNINGS Born in Boston, Lincolnshire, in July 1926 and educated at Oxford High School and St Anne's College, Oxford. She worked at Oxford City Library and then as a reader for Chatto and Windus. Since 1961 she has been a freelance writer and critic, and has won several literary awards for her poetry. She clearly remembers her early interest in poetry at school being fired by good teaching. G. K. Chesterton's *Lepanto* stands out in her memory. She found that travelling, especially in Italy, was an inspiration, as were art and theatre. Elizabeth Jennings lives in Oxford. (SEE p65)

SIDNEY KEYES Born Dartford, Kent, 1922. Educated Tonbridge School and Oxford where he edited *Eight Oxford Poets* with Michael Meyer, who later wrote his memoirs. *The Iron Laurel*, selected poems, appeared in 1942—the same year in which he joined the army. He was taken prisoner at the end of the Tunisian Campaign in April 1943 and died in enemy hands of 'unknown causes'. A highly individual, mature poet, now more widely recognized, he was awarded the Hawthornden Prize posthumously. *Poems* published by Routledge and Keegan Paul. (SEE p83)

LOTTE KRAMER Born in Germany of a Jewish family. Came to England in 1939 as a refugee, but lost many of her family in the holocaust. Worked in a laundry during the war. She studied art and art history at evening classes and still paints and exhibits today. She only began to write and publish poetry in 1970. Her most recent poetry collections are *Icebreak*, *Family Arrivals* and *A Lifelong House*. (SEE p92)

JOHN LATHAM Born 1937, Frodsham, Cheshire. Is a physicist, and works in England and America researching into weather phenomena. He began writing poetry in 1977 and has won major prizes in many national poetry competitions. Several poems have been broadcast on the radio. He lives in Manchester, and two volumes of poetry, *Unpacking Mr Jones* and *From the Other Side of the Street* are published by Peterloo Poets. (SEE p92)

ALUN LEWIS Born Wales, 1915 and went to the University at Aberystwyth. He was a teacher before joining the army as a sapper in the Royal Engineers in 1940. Commissioned in the Infantry and went to India in 1943. Some excellent short war stories were published with some letters in *The Green Bay Tree* (1948). His writing was deeply influenced by Edward Thomas. Alun Lewis emerged as one of the finest Second World War poets, and was killed in Burma on 5th March 1944 on the Arakan Front. *Collected Poems* published by George Allen and Unwin. (SEE pp82, 118, 121, 127)

EILUNED LEWIS Born in Wales. Educated Levana School, Wimbledon and Westfield College, London. On the editorial staff of the *Sunday Times* from 1931–36 and was a regular contributor to *Country Life*. Her best-known books are *Dew on the Grass*, *Leaves on the Tree* and *The Captain's Table*. Also a volume of verse *Morning Songs*. She died in 1970. (SEE p74)

LOUIS MacNEICE Born Belfast, 1907. Educated Sherborne, Marlborough and Merton College, Oxford, where he got a first in Greats and published his first book of poems. Lectured in classics at Birmingham University and Bedford College, London, then joined the BBC features department in 1941 as writer-producer. Wrote many verse plays, also published translations and books of criticism. A volume of autobiography *The Strings are False* appeared in 1965. A diversity of verse forms and a wide range of technical devices make his work memorable. He died in 1963. *Collected Poems* published by Faber. (SEE p64)

ETHEL MANNIN Born 1900 in London. Educated at a local school. She was a prolific novelist, biographer and travel writer, and throughout the war lived in London. She died in 1984. (SEE p99)

LEO MARKS Born 1921. His father was Benjamin Marks, who owned the antiquarian bookshop at 84 Charing Cross Road, which became the subject of a well-known book by Helene Hanff (and now also a film). He was in charge of the Special Operations Executive (SOE) during the war and wrote forty poems that were used by government agents on special missions. (SEE p106)

FRANCES MAYO The poem 'Lament' was published in *New*

Lyrical Ballads published by Editions Poetry London in 1945. (SEE p128)

J. G. MEDDEMMAN The pen name of J. G. Barker. Was a sapper in the Royal Engineers in the Middle East, and after the war worked for British Rail Shipping. (SEE p122)

SPIKE MILLIGAN Born in India in 1918. During the war served with the Royal Artillery in North Africa and Italy. Well-known as a radio, TV and film personality, and an inventive scriptwriter. His special brand of humour was one of the highlights of the Goon Show. Has written several volumes of verse for children, and books on the war which include *Monty: His Part in my Downfall* and *Adolf: My Part in his Downfall*. (SEE p125)

A. A. MILNE (SEE FIRST WORLD WAR)

MAY MORTON Lived in Ulster and worked as a schoolteacher until she retired in 1934. Contributed to various literary magazines and radio programmes in Northern Ireland. (SEE p100)

EDITH PICKTHALL Born 1893 and educated privately. Trained as a midwife and maternity nurse before moving to Mylor, Cornwall, in 1938. She joined the Red Cross Detachment and was involved with treating the ailments of the evacuees. (SEE p78)

JACQUES PRÉVERT Born 1900 in Neuilly-sur-Seine, France. A member of the Surrealist group in Paris for a few years. His collections of poetry include *Paroles*, *Spectacle*, *La pluie et le beau temps* and *Histoires*. He has also written for films and the theatre. (SEE p129)

JOHN PUDNEY Born 1909. Educated Gresham School, Norfolk. A journalist on the *News Chronicle* until the war when he served as a Squadron Leader in the RAF. 'For Johnny' became the most popular poem of the war, and was originally scribbled on the back of an envelope during an air-raid alert in 1941. It was subsequently broadcast, used on radio, and read by Michael Redgrave and John Mills in the film *Way to the Stars*. Much quoted, it has appeared on grave stones and was spoken in the House of Commons in a housing debate. After the nostalgic appeal of much of his war poetry John Pudney progressed to a more complex range in later years. 'For Johnny' was reissued by Shepheard-Walwyn in 1976 and *Selected Poems* is published by Dent (1973). (SEE pp66, 88)

HERBERT READ (SEE FIRST WORLD WAR)

HENRY REED Born 1914. Educated at Birmingham University and was working as a journalist and writer before the war. Joined the Army Ordnance Corps, then worked for the Foreign Office. His war experience inspired the collection *A Map of Verona* (Jonathan Cape) and he wrote some notably original radio plays. (SEE p70)

MICHAEL ROBERTS Born 1902. Educated Bournemouth School, and King's College, London, and Trinity College, Cambridge. Poet, critic, and editor as well as a teacher of maths. Wrote studies on Western civilization, and ecology, and edited *The Faber Book of Modern Verse*. Married the writer Janet Adam Smith. He died in 1948. *Collected Poems*, *Selected Poems and Prose* both published by Carcanet. (SEE p86)

MICHAEL ROSEN Born 1946. Popular children's poet. His latest books include *Hairy Tales and Nursery Crimes* and *Quick, Let's Get Out of Here*, both published by Deutsch. Lives in Hackney, London, with Susanna, Joe, Eddie and two wild frogs in the garden. (SEE p131)

TADEUSZ RÓŻEWICZ Born in 1921 in Radomsko, Poland. Belonged to the Resistance during the war. Writer of poems and short stories. Much of his work—plays and poetry—translated into many languages. He now lives in Wroclaw and is married with two sons. (SEE pp89, 91)

PATRICK SAVAGE Born 1916. Educated Westminster and Christ Church, Oxford. Joined the South Staffordshire Regiment and was a prisoner of war from 1941–45, mostly at Eichstatt camp. A selection of his poetry was published in *Home is the Soldier* (1947). After the war he was headmaster of a school. (SEE p111)

MYRA SCHNEIDER Born 1936 in London but spent most of her childhood during the war years in the Firth of Clyde. Studied English at London University. Has written a children's novel (*Marigold's Monster*) and two novels for teenagers (*If Only I Could*

Walk and *Will the Real Pete Roberts Stand Up?*) all published by Heinemann. Her poems have been published in poetry magazines such as *Pick*, *Pennine Platform* and *Orbis*. (SEE p96)

PAUL SCOTT Born London, 1920. Educated Winchmore Hill Collegiate School. Held a commission in the Indian Army in the Second World War and after the war was a literary agent before becoming a best-selling novelist, and author of *The Raj Quartet*, which was televised as *The Jewel in the Crown* in 1984. Died 1978. (SEE p69)

TORMOD SKAGESTAD Born 1920 in Norway. Some work appears in *Modern Scandinavian Poetry*, edited by Martin Allwood. (SEE p131)

RICHARD SPENDER Born Hereford, 1921, and educated King Edward VI School, Stratford-upon-Avon. Instead of taking up his Oxford scholarship he enlisted in the London Irish Regiment. An officer, he was killed in Tunisia in March 1943, leaving behind a slim volume of poetry published by Sidgwick and Jackson. (SEE p115)

ANTHONY THWAITE Born Chester 1930. Educated at Christ Church, Oxford. Held academic posts in Japan, Libya and Kuwait and was for some years literary editor of the *New Statesman* and the *Listener*, and a BBC radio producer. Co-editor of *Encounter* from 1973–82. As well as many volumes of poetry he has published books of literary criticism, and wrote the Channel 4 series *Six Centuries of Verse*. Married to writer Ann Thwaite, he has four daughters and lives in an old mill house in Norfolk, and in London. (SEE p64)

RUTH TOMALIN Born in County Kilkenny, Ireland. Studied at Chichester High School and King's College, London. She served in the Women's Land Army 1941–2 and then was a staff reporter for various newspapers 1942–65 after which she became freelance. Apart from poetry, she has written novels, children's stories, biographies and works on natural history. (SEE p101)

D. VAN DEN BOGAERDE Born 1921 and educated at University College School, and Allan Glen's School. Served in Europe and the Far East. 'Steel Cathedrals' was first published in 1943 in

Poetry Review; other war poetry appeared in the *Times Literary Supplement*. After the war became well known as the actor, film-star and writer, Dirk Bogarde. (SEE p117)

JOHN WEDGE Born 1921. Served in the Royal Navy during the war, first as a telegraphist in minesweeper *HMS Norse*, then as an officer in *HMS Worcester*, Garlies. After the war he worked for Barclays Bank. (SEE p123)

NIGEL WEIR Born 1919. Educated Winchester and Christ Church, Oxford. Joined the RAF and fought in the Battle of Britain, destroying three enemy planes during the Blitz on 8th August 1940. Awarded the DFC. Killed in action November 1940. *Collected Poems* published by Faber (1941). (SEE p128)

Unfortunately biographical information could not be found on all the poets included in this anthology at the time of going to press. However, the editor and the publishers would be grateful for any information that could be given on the following: May Herschel Clarke; Nina Macdonald; Beatrice Mayor; Erno Muller; and Constance Powell.

ACKNOWLEDGEMENTS

The author and the Publisher would like to thank the following for their kind permission to reprint copyright material in this book:

Susanna Pinney and William Maxwell and Chatto and Windus: The Hogarth Press for 'Black-Out' by Valentine Ackland; Sidgwick & Jackson for 'After the Salvo' by Herbert Asquith; Mrs Nicolete Gray and the Society of Authors on behalf of the Laurence Binyon estate for 'For the Fallen' by Laurence Binyon; The Salamander Oasis Trust for extract from 'Dunkirk' by Basil Bonallack © The Salamander Oasis Trust from *Poems of the Second World War: The Oasis Selection*, published by Dent, Everyman; The Bodley Head for 'Parachute Descent' by David Bourne from *Poems*; The Salamander Oasis Trust for 'Point of View' by R. P. Brett © The Salamander Oasis Trust from *Poems of the Second World War: The Oasis Selection*, published by Dent, Everyman; Paul Berry and Geoffrey Handley-Taylor, Literary Executors of Vera Brittain, for 'Perhaps' and 'Lament of the Demobilized' by Vera Brittain; David Higham Associates Ltd for 'Song of the Dying Gunner' by Charles Causley from *Collected Poems*; Campbell, Connelly & Co Ltd for extract from 'When They Sound the Last All Clear' by Hugh Charles and Louis Elton, copyright © 1941 Dash Music Co Ltd, 78 Newman Street, London W1P 3LA. Reproduced by permission. All rights reserved; Lois Clark for 'Picture from the Blitz' by Lois Clark; Christopher Cornford and Messrs Bircham & Co, Solicitors, for 'Autumn Blitz' by Frances Cornford; Jonathan Cape for 'Will It Be So Again?' by C. Day Lewis from *Collected Poems 1914*; Juliette de Bairacli-Levy for 'Killed in Action' by Juliette de Bairacli-Levy; OUP for 'Simplify Me When I'm Dead' and 'How to Kill' by Keith Douglas © Marie J. Douglas 1978 from *The Complete Poems of Keith Douglas*, edited by Desmond Graham (1978); Penny Drinkwater for 'Nineteen-Fifteen' by John Drinkwater; David Higham Associates Ltd for 'Easter Monday (In Memoriam Edward Thomas, 1917)' by Eleanor Farjeon from *First and Second Love* by Eleanor Farjeon; Joan Farjeon for 'Even Hitler Had a Mother' by Herbert Farjeon; Karen Gershon for 'In Every Street' from *Collected Poems* by Karen Gershon, published by Gollancz; Macmillan and OUP for 'Battle', 'Shells', The Bull', and 'When the Plane Dived' by W. W. Gibson; Macmillan for 'Mangel Worzels', 'His Mate', 'Breakfast' and 'Back' by W. W. Gibson, from *Collected Poems 1905–1925*; Virginia Thesiger and *Punch* for 'For This Relief', 'Losing Face' and 'Autumn Leaves' by Virginia Graham; A. P. Watt Ltd on behalf of the Executors of the Estate of Robert Graves for 'The Leveller' and 'Corporal Stare' by Robert Graves from *Fairies and Fusiliers*; Redwood Music Ltd, 129 Park Street, London, W1Y 3FA for 'If I Were the Only Girl in the World', words by Clifford Grey; Robin Haines for

159

knights Press; David Higham Associates Ltd for 'Praematuri' and 'The Falling Leaves' by Margaret Postgate Cole from *Poems*; David Higham Associates Ltd for 'Empty Your Pockets' and 'For Johnny' by John Pudney from *Poems*; David Higham Associates Ltd for 'The Execution of Cornelius Vane' and 'Aeroplanes' by Herbert Read from *Poems*; Jonathan Cape for 'Naming of Parts' by Henry Reed from *A Map of Verona*; Carcanet Press Ltd for 'Winter Warfare' by Edgell Rickword from *Behind the Eyes: Collected Poems and Translations* (1976); Carcanet Press Ltd for 'The Child' by Michael Roberts from *Selected Poems and Prose*, edited by Frederick Grubb (1980); André Deutsch for 'Pebble' by Michael Rosen from *Quick, Let's Get Out of Here*; Anvil Press Poetry Ltd for 'Pigtail' and 'Massacre of the Boys' by Tadeusz Różewicz from *Conversation With the Prince*, translated by Adam Czerniawski, published by Anvil Press Poetry (1982); Chappell Music for extract from 'Your King and Country Want You' by Paul Rubens © 1914 Chappell Music Ltd. Reproduced by permission; George Sassoon for 'The Dug Out', 'Suicide in the Trenches', 'Reconciliation', 'The Death Bed', 'Does it Matter' and 'Aftermath' by Siegfried Sassoon; Charles Skilton Ltd for 'Second Autumn' by Patrick Savage from *Home is the Soldier*, published by the Fortune Press, Charles Skilton Ltd; Vernon Scannell for 'The Great War' by Vernon Scannell; Myra Schneider, *Fistful of Yellow Hope* (Littlewood Press) and *Chaos of the Night* edited by Catherine Reilly (Virago) for 'Drawing a Banana' by Myra Schneider; David Higham Associates Ltd for 'Tell Us the Tricks' by Paul Scott from *Poets Now*, published by Heinemann; Martin Allwood for 'The Year After' by Tormod Skagestad, translated by Martin Allwood from *Modern Scandinavian Poetry*, Anglo-American Center, Mullsjö, Sweden, 1982; Sidgwick and Jackson for 'Weekend Leave' by Richard Spender from *Collected Poems 1943*; Anthony Thwaite for 'Bournemouth, September 3rd, 1939' by Anthony Thwaite; Ruth Tomalin for 'Ladybird, Ladybird' by Ruth Tomalin; A. D. Peters & Co Ltd for 'Steel Cathedrals' by D. van den Bogaerde; The Salamander Oasis Trust for 'Still No Letter' by John Wedge © The Salamander Oasis Trust from *Poems of the Second World War: The Oasis Selection*, published by Dent, Everyman; Faber and Faber for 'War' by A. N. C. Weir from *Verses of a Fighter Pilot*; Mrs Lesley Weissenborn for linocut illustration by Hellmuth Weissenborn © 1987 Lesley Weissenborn; Miss Ann Wolfe for 'A Thrush in the Trenches' by Humbert Wolfe; A. P. Watt Ltd on behalf of Michael B. Yeats and Macmillan, London Ltd for 'An Irish Airman Foresees His Death' by W. B. Yeats from *The Collected Poems of W. B. Yeats*.

Every effort has been made to trace the copyright holders but the author and Publishers apologise if any inadvertent omission has been made.